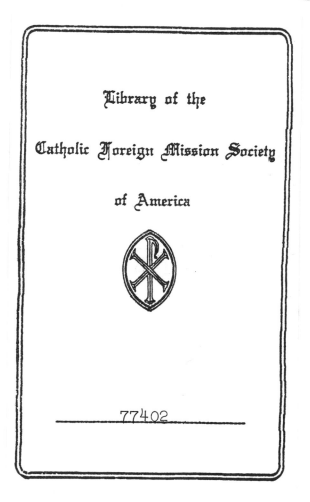

God and Politics

God and Politics

R. L. Bruckberger

Translated from the French by Eleanor Levieux

J. Philip O'Hara, Inc. · Chicago

© 1971 Librairie Plon

J. Philip O'Hara, Inc. 20 East Huron, Chicago, 60611.
Published simultaneously in Canada by Van Nostrand
Reinhold Ltd., Scarborough, Ontario.

Library of Congress Cataloging in Publication Data

Bruckberger, Raymond Leopold, 1907-
    God and politics.

    "A Howard Greenfeld book."
    Translation of Dieu et la politique.
    1. Christianity and politics. 2. Revolution
(Theology) 3. Church and state—Catholic Church.
I. Title.
BR115.P7B69713   261.7   78-190754
ISBN 0-87955-302-2

First Printing I

A Howard Greenfeld Book

Contents

T o the memory
of Cardinal Jules-Géraud Salièges,
Archbishop of Toulouse,
former superior of the Grand Séminaire de Saint-Flour,
who discerned my Dominican vocation
and encouraged me to follow it,
in fervent homage to the admirable example
which he left the Clergy of France:
example of strength of character and non-conformism,
faithfulness to the Church and to his country,
fraternal devotion to the poor
and the persecuted.
. With heartfelt thanks.

R. L. B.
July 25, 1971,
35th anniversary of my
ordination in the priesthood

"I do not by any means despair of the future. The handful of men who, on a world scale, represent a country like ours, may very well play the role, tomorrow, in relation to the materialistic civilization which is collapsing, which was played in 1940 by another handful of men, in relation to deliquescent Vichy France. But first of all, our people must be helped to rid themselves of a certain number of lies which, far from sustaining their pride, ultimately make them disgusted with themselves, because they no longer believe them."

Georges Bernanos
January 22, 1948

God and Politics

Letter to the American People, by Way of A Preface

I like the way Americans have of introducing themselves, saying simply who they are, and reminding you, if necessary, when they've met you before. It saves time and makes conversation clearer.

It's already more than twenty years since I "discovered" America. That was in the early summer of 1950. I arrived by sea, on board the "Ile de France." Those who arrive by air today cannot imagine what a tremendous shock it was, after spending several days on an empty ocean, to see the tall skyline of Manhattan rise out of the sea and come to meet you. New York, said Céline, is a city that greets you standing up. There you have the very image of your country, America, a country standing on its feet, on the move, walking toward the future with wide-open eyes. Through the illusion created by the speed of the boat, I saw that country standing up, moving toward me to welcome me. It was the great America, the beautiful, the mysterious America, the new continent to be discovered.

The Korean War had just begun. In the wake of so many immigrants, I arrived, weary of Europe, knowing nothing but wanting to know about the enormous mystery that pulsates deep inside your continent. I loved America, loved it deeply and even today, after so many years, my heart is flooded with gratitude for everything it gave me. America stands up to greet you. In case you had been feeling like lying down, that forces you to straighten up and look it right in the eye. America puts people on their feet, makes them stand up. America made me stand up and I've remained standing. I don't feel like lying down at all any more. I won't lie down until I die.

Between the Korean War and President Nixon's trip to Peking, what a lot of distance has been covered! But it's not politics that I want to talk about. Fortunately, it is for reasons other than political ones that I love America. It seems to me there is not much difference between Nixon in Peking and Roosevelt at Yalta. Each of those two presidents undoubtedly did what was in his best interest. But too many innocent people the world over pay for the election campaigns of American presidents. It's become a ritual part of United States domestic politics. Now, with a presidential re-election coming up, one could even invent a game which would consist of guessing which people on this earth, which one of the United States' faithful allies, will have to pay for the re-election of the president.

At the time of the Suez business, in 1956, it was Israel, France and England, then the Hungarian people, who paid for Eisenhower's re-election. This time, the round of publicity preceding Nixon's re-election was paid for by the Chinese of Formosa. It is possible that those Chinese may pay very dearly for that re-election. Granted, perhaps their situation was absurd; but this could have been realized a great deal earlier. What strikes me is that people all around me are beginning to talk about Formosa the way, in 1938, at the time of Munich, people in Paris talked about the Czechs, and the way I heard them talk, the following year, about Poland and the Dantzig Corridor. In French we have a saying: "Whoever wants to drown his dog says it has rabies." Strange, how quickly the innocent are suspected of having rabies as soon as it becomes useful and convenient to drown them. It is not always pleasant, being America's dog.

International politics is surely one area where the fallen nature of man is clearly apparent. It is one of the areas where it is the most difficult to do good, to do only good, and to avoid evil. There is almost always one side of every political action which is unjust, which injures innocent people and betrays allies. It is better to face the fact that human nature is powerless, crippled in that way, better to recognize

these flaws and give them the names they deserve—
original sin, wound of fallen nature—than to camouflage and try to justify them.

W hat makes a nation a Christian one has
nothing to do with power, prosperity, or
wealth. Success in temporal matters is even an ob-
stacle to the spirit of the Gospel. Not always, however. Simone Weil said that justice was always a fugi-
tive from the winners' side. I think she was exag-
gerating, as she was in the habit of doing; for after all,
the dazzling American victory of 1945 took the entire world under its wings, freeing many innocent
people. The pity of it is that that victory did not
extend still further and that at Yalta, the President of
the United States, abetted by England, rejected the
opportunity to carry the liberating shadow of those
wings of victory right up to the frontiers of old
Russia. As a result, the very same countries for whose
freedom that war had been fought—Poland, Czech-
oslovakia, all of eastern Europe—ended up more en-
slaved after the war than before it.

The responsibilities of nations, especially when
they are powerful nations, are awesome. For over a
hundred years, your country, America, was a self-
appointed refuge, located outside history and its contradictions; then, without transition, you Americans

began to determine the course of history and its contradictions, for the entire world. America now is part of the minds and hearts of billions of human beings all over the planet. Just the name "America" itself sparks some feeling or idea in every single Chinese or Russian, every Hungarian or Israeli, every Frenchman or German, every Congolese or Vietnamese, every Brazilian or Japanese.

This does not mean that the image each of us has of your country is always very accurate, or very favorable, but that's quite another matter. What is new, what was not even foreseeable a hundred years ago—except by certain exceptionally lucid men like de Tocqueville—is the fact that your country is present today in the minds of the entire human species. An enormous responsibility!

I cannot begin to tell you how much food for thought there is in the history of the world these last thirty years, especially in the history of your country.

It has happened at least twice in the course of history that the burden of "world leadership," as you call it and as the whole world calls it along with you, has fallen on the shoulders of a great people, who were not expecting it, were not prepared for it, had never sought it, and did not want it. It happened to Rome, and it happened to you, America. But possessing world leadership is one thing; knowing what to do with it is another. When a universal responsibility unexpectedly comes along, one has to be genuinely at ease with oneself, to take it in stride.

L et's not talk about China. No one really knows
what is going on there, no one knows the real
principles by which that enormous mass of men and
women lives, acts and dies. No one knows to what
extent, exactly, the ancient Chinese civilization has
survived in the new mores and the new social organization of that vast country. The invasion, conquest
and military occupation of Tibet in the spring of
1959 leave some doubt as to the liberal and peaceful
nature of that regimented society.

But what of Russia? Where power is concerned, it
is an inflexible country, that does not loosen its grip
on the countries it has conquered. Some countries,
and Russia is one of them, are greedy for domination
the way some individuals are greedy for money; they
do not let go of it easily. But that is not the strangest
part. Where Russia is concerned, there is far more to
it. Its domination is nurtured and spread by an
ideology, an implacable political orthodoxy: Hegel's
philosophy, completed by Marxism-Leninism.

In a sense, nothing is finer or more admirable than
the alliance of military strength with philosophy.
Such an alliance has several times existed, with the
most fortunate results. It alone can explain the mas-
sive conquests which have burst on the world like
transfigurations. Such was the conquest, for instance,
of all the Orient by Alexander the Great. His military
genius and the Macedonian army were the vehicles of
Hellenism, for which all the young people throughout
the known world at that time burned with enthusiasm. Now, of course, it was military strength

which broke down the barriers, but had it not been for the vigorous appeal of Greek art and thought, Alexander's dazzling victories would have trickled away like water in sand. Hellenism was a veritable liberation of the mind, a burgeoning of the soul, and all of these peoples felt this so keenly that they gratefully embraced the Greek way of life and the Greek way of thinking and, although conquered in battle, they never considered themselves defeated but instead felt liberated, promoted to a higher rank of civilization. What a marvelous adventure, for a youth living in Ecbatana in the year 330 BC, to discover—through the glory of a handsome and fabulously lucky young general — Sophocles and Phidias, Praxiteles and Plato.

Until then, these populous tribes, countless as the Chinese today, had known nothing but the confusion of the masses or the primitive hierarchy of clan structure, the cheapness of life on the human ant heap or the tyranny of one man over others, and had feared cruel deities lusting for human blood. Suddenly, behind Alexander, emerged the profile of Antigone, the unique worth of the individual, distinctions as to form and style, untrammeled intelligence, order born of wit and embodied in fine materials.

That was certainly enough to fill the young with enthusiasm. Even when the great conquests originate in a military victory, they continue and last only if they free minds and win hearts. That particular conquest was to last a millenium and a half, ending only with the fall of Constantinople in 1453. Anyone who does not look on 1453 as marking a sinister bereavement has never known what the word "civilization" means.

Thanks to Alexander's conquests, the expansion of Hellenism, then the Pax Romana, Christianity was able, in turn, and in the space of a few centuries, to elevate man and conquer what was then the known world. No matter what periods of collapse, decadence, regression there may have been, despite the long tunnels which you term "the dark ages," one has the feeling that mankind has been slowly climbing toward greater spiritual enlightenment, a fuller harmony of morals, a more heroic character. Throughout the centuries the trial of Joan of Arc has echoed the dialogue of Antigone; Francis of Assisi has brought us memories of Orpheus; Thomas Aquinas has revived Aristotle (whom he rediscovered through the Arabs); Liszt and Stravinsky have retrieved folk melodies from reminiscences of remotest antiquity; while thousands of saints, whether glorious or obscure, have unceasingly reminded the world of the warnings of the Prophets of Israel, Jesus' sacrifice on the Cross, and the triumph of love and hope in the renewed affirmation of the resurrection. What is common to all this and is still capable of enchanting the heart is the day-by-day ascension of light on the horizon, the way man constantly outdoes man in genius and devotion. Every morning the sun rises again, every morning everything is to be done all over again, and every morning men get on their feet again to pray, talk, write and act. Prayer is supreme. A civilization that no longer knows how to pray has lost its center of gravity. But it is important not to confuse prayer with pointless chitchat or the contemplation of one's own navel. Prayer is essentially an elevation of the soul toward God transcendant.

What will become of the Western world? It is beginning to lose its faith in itself. Like the Roman Empire before it, the West is starting to experience self-doubt, just at the moment of its loftiest triumph. The wars and the victories you Americans won simply speeded up the triumphal process, so that your victories, Americans, were those of the entire West. So it is only right that you should be the first to hesitate, the first to begin to feel self-doubt. What we found discouraging about you, for a long time, was that you did not seem to feel any self-doubt. Now you are beginning to doubt yourselves, and you're doing it in your own, rather devastating way. What most people take as a sign of weakness, I interpret as a justification of hope. Military strength often plays a prophetic role. That war in Vietnam that you have not lost but are incapable of

winning has faced you with a question about yourselves, about your own legitimacy and the legitimacy
of your power and your leadership. Blessed be that
questioning! Barbarians and imbeciles never experience self-doubt.

After all, something very astonishing has happened. For the time being, all of the world's
religions are merely surviving themselves. They have
been so heavily assaulted, over the past two centuries,
and undergone so severe a shock that they have been
shaken right down to the roots and the core. Even
though many people do not want to see the obvious,
and still less acknowledge it, the religions are coasting
on their own inertia, using automatic gestures and
habits, but they have really taken on an air of som-
nambulism, sleeping as they walk along the edge of
the roof.

The religions are mere survivals of themselves because they have actually been replaced, in the
people's hearts, by a purely materialistic civilization,
geared solely to the conquest and exploitation of
nature and the organization of the universe, the goal
being to keep man comfortable and amused.
Marxism-Leninism gets along just fine with this materialistic civilization; it is the adequate and ideal expression of that civilization. But Christianity cannot

help but be out of plumb with respect to such a civilization, which beheads man of his dimension: eternity. The misunderstanding of the Western world is that its civilization no longer agrees with its religion, or that its religion is no longer in gear with its civilization.

The West's real missionaries — the ones who converted the entire world—have been machines, medical science and audio-visual techniques. Thanks to these, not only were all the witch doctors beaten on their own home ground, stripped of their powers and of the prestige which attached to those powers, but in fact the Western, material civilization appeared to the primitive peoples as the supreme Sorcery; the least little scientist or engineer became the sorcerer of sorcerers. Once the first astonishment was over, there was the enchantment of discovering that, best of all, the sorcery of the Western world wore no mask, had no secrets from the other peoples, detested secrets, in fact; Western witchcraft was prepared to initiate one and all into the origins of its power, and even maintained that everyone could be taught to wield it. It offered itself as an explanation of the world and claimed to satisfy the mind.

Whereupon the primitive peoples were buoyed up by an enormous hope. They looked on our Western civilization as sorcery-for-all, the universal do-it-yourself of material progress and the domination of the age-old forces of nature which until then had aroused only terror in them. A tremendous liberation! But even more tremendous still, perhaps, what a misunderstanding!

How is it that in 1946, after your staggering, total victory extending beyond two oceans, after your enemies' unconditional surrender, an American citizen could go all the way around the world and be received everywhere like a king? And that twenty-five years later you are being kept at bay almost everywhere throughout the world, so that you are tempted to withdraw entirely within your own borders, and at times you are even detested by peoples whom you helped to liberate?

It is true: you are not very well liked. But then, what people is? The French are prone to believe that they are liked and that foreigners are dazzled by them; they are deluding themselves.

Anyhow, things come and go. As with individuals, so with nations: they are sometimes liked, sometimes detested. France in the days of King Louis IX was loved and admired. The French king was made prisoner in Spain, stripped of everything, dying—and chosen to arbitrate the quarrels between Princes of the nation that was holding him captive.

France in the days of the French Revolution was loved — passionately loved — and is still loved today by many poor souls throughout the world who picture it through the novels of Victor Hugo. The French Revolution fascinated men on a universal scale, including geniuses like Beethoven and Goethe. Napoleon appeared as the heir to that revolution: there is no other explanation possible for his military gains. Everywhere in Europe, the French were welcomed as liberators. Then their victory wore thin and

Napoleon was defeated, not so much by Wellington's genius as by the lassitude of Europe itself.

There are also opportunities that are lost for lack of willingness to perceive them. In 1945, at the time of the Allies' victory over the Axis countries, England, Russia and America had everything they needed to be passionately loved. The peoples of the world spontaneously held out to them their gratitude and admiration. But England does not want to be loved; it is the least coquettish of nations.

Russia is not coquettish either. But it is greedy. Its advantage is that since 1917 it has, like the French Revolution, possessed a formula for prestige throughout the world, namely: Marxism-Leninism, which claims to be a "scientific" ideology, capable of solving all social problems and immediately procuring men's happiness here on earth. Whether that is true is another matter. But the fact is that for more than half a century, Russia has stirred the devotion of humble people throughout the world; very often, for Russia's sake, they have betrayed their own country. Most of these traitors, in fact, were so convinced of the legitimacy of the Soviet messianism that they did not feel they were betraying anything. And when they were punished for treason, they proclaimed that they were martyrs, martyrs to the great cause of the people's liberation.

A merica's victory was infinitely greater, more extensive, more decisive than Russia's; especially, more than England's. It was really America that won the Second World War, and won it at every point on the planet. Twenty-five years later, we are entitled to note, and to say, that America has lost that overwhelming victory. It has lost it, not the way one loses a battle but rather, inadvertently, without knowing how it happened, the way one loses some object—an umbrella or a key. America has lost its victory, mislaid it; America doesn't know—nobody knows—where that overwhelming victory has gone.

There is something very irritating, even scandalous, about the way it has been mislaid. In 1945 it seemed as though America possessed everything it needed to dominate the world, be its leader. It even made a magnanimous effort to provide the leadership that was thrust upon it, without its having sought such a role. It put its former enemies back on their feet. The way America held out its hand to its former enemies and helped them to stand up again remains a glorious example of generosity that may be unique in history.

As for Europe, it was the Marshall Plan that saved it from Communism. Or rather, to put it more precisely, the Marshall Plan saved it from the poverty which makes Communism so keenly, and as if irresistibly, tempting. The Marshall Plan restored to Europe its own freedom, the possibility of choosing its own destiny, its own course. Which does not mean that Europe is entirely out of danger, even where Communism is concerned. But before the Marshall

Plan, it was almost inevitable that Europe succumb to
it. Should Europe succumb to it tomorrow, this
would no longer be an inevitability but, instead, the
effect of its refusal to assume its own responsibilities.
How striking it is that to today's Western conscience,
Communism appears as the abdication of all spiritual
expectation.

That is just where America missed the boat. It is
because your country's spiritual dimension was not
apparent to the peoples of the world that, ultimately,
you did not win their hearts. When someone has lived
right in the middle of the United States for eight
years, as I did, he knows that that spiritual dimension
does exist; he knows to what extent the citizens and
the collectivities of America are imbued with Christianity and a very original concept of individual dignity and political freedom. But this was not obvious
outside the States. Your wealth and prodigality dazzled the world, but it did not seem as through you
had any soul. That is what I so strongly hold against
your great writers: they are read throughout the
world, but they were not able, or willing, to tell the
world what kind of heart and spirit you have. People
concluded that you didn't have any. You were envied, but you were not loved.

The grave question which arises (and the mere fact
that it does arise is disturbing) is actually this: will
the Western world survive, since it no longer seems to
have any reason to go on living? After all, it is not the
material reasons—the economic prosperity and the
power—that suffice to justify men in living, in ob-
serving themselves live, in loving to live, in giving

thanks. To the query, "Why was man created and brought into the world?", the traditional Christian teaching replied by confronting each man with the ultimates: God, eternity, the Last Judgment, love of one's fellow man for God's sake. But our modern civilization, geared exclusively to dominating nature, producing material goods, making man comfortable in this world, has lost sight of the ultimates. It is even helping marvelously to distract man from them, to teach him to do without them.

Now, a civilization begins to decline when any end, no matter which, justifies any means, no matter which. If war has taught us anything, it has certainly taught us that. But a civilization is in the final stages of decay when the means are in the final stages of replacing the very order of the ultimates.

There is no longer any hope, in this world or the next—not only for America but for the entire world, and I do not exclude either Russia or China—except in a spiritual resurrection, the rediscovery of what is most transcendant and most intimate in man and which is the image of God, sealed within him in the first morning of the world.

Easter 1972
R.L. Bruckberger

Part 1

Double
Allegiance

Summer was off to a superb start. The sky was clear, the weather hot. It was the 28th of June; the date is marked in all the history books. I was a very small boy, just seven. I remember everything better than if it had been yesterday. I know very well why all the details of that scene, including the words I didn't understand, are so deeply and accurately engraved on my memory.

It was late afternoon in that little town in Auvergne. My father was sitting with friends at the terrace of a café. He had taken me along with him, and I was concentrating on drinking a glass of fruit syrup and water, with a drop of *cassis* in it. The weather was really beautiful. Suddenly a girl came running across the square toward us. We knew her very well; she lived in the house over the café; she was the telegraph operator at the post office in our little

town. She came closer and said to my father, "Archduke Francis Ferdinand has been assassinated in Sarajevo!" My father went pale, his eyes filled with tears.
That was the only time in my life I ever saw my
father cry. He was married to a Frenchwoman and
the father of five young children, but by birth and
nationality he was Austrian, and he loved the House
of Hapsburg. "This means war . . ." he said. He got
up and went alone into the café. I don't remember
what happened immediately afterward. Everyone
knows what followed throughout the world.

Those words that were so strange to the ears of a
small French boy — Sarajevo, Francis Ferdinand,
Archduke, assassination — what did they convey to
me? I had seen my father cry; he had pronounced the
word "war." I was the kind of little boy who likes to
fight; war for me was a matter of wooden swords.
Certainly that was nothing to cry about. (There
would be no lack of opportunities, as time went by,
to revise that hasty judgment.) Abruptly, that word
"war," along with my father's tears, made me feel
that a sudden, invisible, monstrous, unavoidable presence was menacing us all, that a cataclysm was erupt-
ing in our world and would lay it waste like fire, like
an avalanche, like lightning, like an earthquake for
which no one was responsible but which was going to
upset the destiny of each and every person.

In the middle of that burning summer afternoon, I
had received a revelation of what politics was, although of course I did not know that that was its
name.

I apologize to the reader for beginning this book

on God and politics with a personal recollection, and a childhood memory at that, the meaning of which is still open to debate, whereas the topic of this book would seem to call for more solemn and abstract treatment. But that is just the point; right from the outset, I want to lift my topic out of abstraction and solemnity. God is not an abstract subject. And as for politics, we are all in a good position to know, in this latter part of the twentieth century, that that is no abstract subject either. It is a frightening subject, dripping with human blood and pain. Shoving live children into a crematory oven — that is politics, and that is not abstract. When I think back on all the sights which the professional politicians have given us to see in the course of my lifetime, I am reminded of a nightmare that poor Gerard Nerval described this way more than a century ago: "Separated by steel, they meet in a hideous kiss, sealed by the blood of men." Only for us it was not a nightmare. We were not dreaming.

We have lived through horror after horror. At the same time, my generation has experienced the most disappointing of intellectual adventures. The word "adventure" itself is too strong; "routine" is what we must call it.

Ever since Napoleon I and Goya's "Disasters of the

War," we have watched history move faster and faster toward the horrors of war, police brutality, man's hatred for man. One would have thought the Nazi concentration camps had wrought horror to an unsurpassable pitch, to the level of a masterpiece. One would have thought all this might make us stop and think and even—who knows?—thoroughly overhaul our scale of values, our conception of life, our philosophical systems, the very bases of what we still dare to call our civilization. One would have thought that having emerged miraculously from the inferno, Europe would try to exorcise its monsters, probe its conscience, earnestly investigate how and why it had come to that, had fallen into that appalling situation where crime formed an endless chain, where each lie engendered a dozen more and fear dishonored the very light of day.

But no, not at all. Nothing of the kind!

We have turned the concentration camps into memorials where chiefs of state deposit wreaths of flowers; we make sure that the military cemeteries are well-kept and tidy; every year we have one or two more national holidays, especially welcome when they fall on a Friday or a Monday, as that gives us a long weekend when we can take madly to the highways. But our journalists and writers and philosophy professors and political theorists and party leaders have begun snoring again in their gentle intellectual way, picking up right where they left off. Not the slightest attempt to question the validity of anything . . .

Technology is making prodigious leaps forward.

Man has walked on the moon. We have invented the end of the world and we are keeping it in storage in our arsenals. When I die one day, it may be with a heart that is not my own—as has already happened to one of my Brothers. But the ideological museum of modern man remains unchanged beneath age-old layers of dust. And yet . . .

At the end of the last century, Pope Leo XIII wrote an admirable Encyclical called *Aeterni Patris* which, read with the hindsight of two world wars, can be seen as a prophetic warning, an unheeded warning. I beg the reader to read these lines from it with his fullest attention: "If we consider the evil genius of the times, if our thoughts embrace the state of both public and private affairs, we easily discern the cause of the evils which overwhelm us and of those which threaten us. It is this: mistaken opinions about human and divine things, produced by the philosophical schools, have spread through all ranks of society and have ultimately come to be accepted by a great many minds. It is natural for man to be guided by the lights of his reason. Wherefore the errors of the mind are inevitably reflected in failings of will. The falseness of our thinking influences our conduct and makes it depraved. Whereas a sound intelligence which rests firmly on true and solid principles is for both society and the individual the source of great advantages and countless benefits."

In these terms this liberal Pope, who sensed the oncoming storms, attributed the miseries of men directly to a sickness of the mind. Although I have never cared very much for Charles Maurras, I have

always liked the Provencal proverb he was fond of
quoting: "Fish rot from the head down!"

But there is nothing more difficult than to make
men give some salutary thought to the defects of
their judgment. It is a well-known fact that everyone
complains of his memory playing tricks on him but
no one complains of his judgment. We care more
about our ideas than we do about life—about other
people's lives, especially. What difference do millions
of people killed make to us? What difference do
atrocities, or tortures, or totalitarian regimes make?
We are ready to ascribe these catastrophes to any old
cause at all, just so long as we ourselves are not
obliged to question the philosophies or prejudices
that are dear to us, that we live on, and whose ac-
complices we are. We revile Hitler and Stalin—and yet
they were nothing more than good students of
philosophers whom we revere and whose theories and
whose scorn of men they candidly applied. So, as
long as the mind has not stopped to give some critical
thought to itself, what chance can we have of halting
the rotting process and restoring health?

All of us have our share of responsibility in this
state of affairs—all of us: Christians and other people,
Christians more than other people. In the days of
Leo XIII, the young Catholic clergy was not completely given over to the intellectual fashion of the
times. It was still aware of guarding a treasure-trove
of truths that were shocking for the period, quite at
variance with the philosophies current then but
which, pitted against all of those philosophies together and their harmful consequences, were capable

of restoring health to man and society. Now this safety catch has been broken. Just as the most lucid minds are beginning to doubt the wisdom of those philosophies and ideologies which have been dominating the world and setting the fashion for the past two centuries, at the same time the most energetic and noisy, if not the most dynamic, segment of the clergy in the Western world is literally stampeding towards the leading conformist slogans, the fixed ideas, the outstanding prejudices. Saint Paul said, "And be not conformed to this world!", but Saint Paul's exhortation seems to be crossed out of the Scriptures. Might as well try to remind a huge flock of zealous geese of those words, as they go waddling along with outstretched necks, in their haste to run after the first fowl that happens by. Priests forever, after the Order of Malchisedec, as the liturgy says: how very sad . . .

Hegel said that ideas are living things; meaning, I suppose, that they are born, grow, develop, assimilate the surrounding environment, produce waste products, age, and die. Now, if, on the other hand, it is ideas which make the earth go round, then it seems to me that we should be able clearly to see in what direction the ideas that have made the earth go round for more than two centuries have turned it. It seems to me that we should be entitled to exact some accounts from them.

I dream of a Nuremberg trial for ideas, including Hegel's own ideas. They would be summoned to appear in court, where they would be given the opportunity to account for themselves, to defend themselves if possible, but where they would be sentenced if they deserved to be sentenced. I doubt that the most criminal among them could be hanged—but one should be able to place them in the pillory and publish the grounds for their punishment.

After all, why should ideas alone be allowed to shirk all responsibility? Why should they never be judged? That would really be asking a little too much. Hitler and the grand *condottieri* who were hanged at Nuremberg were not, after all, the products of spontaneous generation; they did not just suddenly materialize on stage, as if by magic. Neither did Stalin and his security agents. They are the natural—I was about to say, the necessary—products of our Western society. All these fine specimens are specimens of our world; their ideas were the ideas you find lying about everywhere, in books, in the newspapers, in conversation; only, they had the power and the naïveté to apply them thoroughly in real life. As Giraudoux put it, it is from the naïve that you fashion monsters. Every psychiatrist, every criminologist knows that. I have observed it myself a hundred times in the course of my life. And when a monster comes to power, he uses that power as naturally as can be. There was always something childlike in Hitler's gaze.

It is possible that each era thinks it is worse than

all those that have gone before. As far as you are concerned, nothing worse can happen than what happens to you. For a long time, however, the Middle Ages were considered a particularly cruel and barbarous period. Today we do not quite dare to say that anymore, for then what should we say about our own period?

Our own period does evil efficiently; perhaps that is what is genuinely original about it. That is also how it overwhelms and subdues intelligence. Efficiency on a gigantic scale is its moral alibi. We are impressed by technology, taking it as the alpha and the omega of any justification. A hired assassin who stabbed someone at a street corner was a criminal. But the pilot who dropped the bomb on Hiroshima from 15,000 feet up—how are we supposed to label him? He was acting on orders, he went out of his mind because of them. His act was too enormous for his human brain to encompass.

For instance, there is absolutely nothing new about looking on lies as a systematic means of taking and keeping power. Machiavelli lived a long time ago, and he in turn was part of a tradition older than himself. What is new is that lies, termed propaganda, can be spread so widely, pounded so hard into so many brains, that any imposter, no matter who, can fanaticize an entire people—as we saw in the case of Hitler and Goebbels.

There is absolutely nothing new about eliminating the people who do not think the way the government does. The Inquisition practiced such elimination and perfected it at the end of the Middle Ages, and the

Terror did the same in France. But the Terror in France and the Inquisition in Spain, where it raged the most, produced only a few thousand victims (which is of course too many as it is). What is new is that citizens are denounced on an industrial scale and police inquisition can control entire classes of society. And this is only the beginning. Once data-processing and computers have started to control men, the existence of an independent thought anywhere may well become merely an idle dream.

With horror, history has recorded a number of frightful burnings at the stake—the Cathars at Montségur, the Knights Templar, Joan of Arc, and many more. What is new is that industrialization of burning at the stake, that mass-produced holocaust called crematory ovens capable of gulping down millions of men, women, and children and turning them into smoke.

With horror, history has recorded appalling massacres—the Sicilian Vespers, Saint Bartholomew's Day, the extermination of the Irish by the English, of the Armenians by the Turks. What is new is the industrialization of genocide, modestly called "final solution," which has made mere survivors of the Jews and the gypsies.

History tells us how cities have been sacked. But what is the sack of a city compared with the nuclear weapon, which razes a metropolis in a flash?

What I am saying here may be a commonplace by now, but that does not make it any less atrocious. We must go all the way, as one American scientist has done, claiming that the novelty is the possibility of collective suicide. All that is necessary is that four or five men in the world push four or five buttons—and all the other men will cease to exist. And we owe this novelty to science.

Nothing, you see, can stop progress. Now it is the entire species that you can wipe out with just one blow. In any case, this scientist is wrong on one point—perhaps involuntarily, but the error is certainly significant. If those four or five buttons were pushed all at once and if the catastrophe occurred, causing the human race to disappear, this would definitely not be a collective suicide: this would still be murder. Where there is suicide there is necessarily the consent of the person who dies. But no one is going to ask us for our consent.

What difference does it make? you will say; if this happens, there won't be anyone around to decide who is responsible. But it is right now, now while there is still time, that things must be clarified. If this is a case of potential murder, why not look for the potential murderers in advance, so as at least to keep an eye on them? People are put under surveillance on the strength of much less serious possibilities than that. If we "owe this novelty to science," then I should think it would be prudent to keep science and scientists under close surveillance.

Now, this particular American scientist comes to the opposite conclusion. He wants someone to explain to him by what miracle the problems created by science could be solved in any way that overlooks the scientific method. Politics are a leftover of the pre-scientific age, he says, and the political class is the last feudal power. Our so-called political problems can be solved only by the scientific method—or not at all. If not at all, that means suicide. So the first thing to do is get rid of the politicians and everything that operates through them.

This American scientist is a Nobel Prize winner—another one of those naïve men of whom monsters are made.

While I am not in the least a prophet, yet solely through the dialetic of such examples of so-called scientific reasoning, I predict that the world will very shortly go through an era of *pronunciamentos*. But this time it is not the army officers who will bring off the *coups d'état;* real power no longer lies with the army. These *pronunciamentos* will come from the scientists, who of course know a thousand times better than we do what is good for us, and who now have the means to force it down our throats. I further predict that even the fiercest of military dictatorships will have been paradise on earth compared to the scientific dictatorships whose advent this gentle American scientist seems to be announcing.

The time may very well come, and quickly too, at that, when the scientists' undertakings will be even more dangerous for what remains of Western civilization than the barbarian invasions were for the declining Roman Empire. The barbarians at least were still human beings. But the scientists . . .

S o, what we owe to science and the scientists is
    not so much the possibility of collective suicide
as the weapon (four or five buttons) capable of exterminating the entire human race with one blow, and
doubtless all life as well, including the race to which
we owe everything, hope supreme and supreme
thought—the monkeys. And they come and tell us
that only the arms manufacturer who has produced
this marvelous exterminating machine should have
charge of preventing the murder—by continuing to
use his own method. I do not understand this reasoning. By what miracle is it precisely the arms manu-
facturers who could prevent the use of the arms they
have developed and supplied to the potential murderers? It is not customary for the gunsmith, when he
sells one of his weapons, to provide the client with
instructions on how not to use it.

Perhaps science and the scientists could come up
with a device which would instantly cause lightning
to strike whoever tried to push one of those four or
five buttons. We would be grateful to them if they
would. But things do not seem to be heading in that
direction. It is because of science that we are in danger of being collectively assassinated. It is because of
science that we are in imminent danger of seeing the
world come to an end. It is very unlikely that science
will succeed in saving us from a peril for which it is
responsible in the first place and which it alone has
created.

Staggering situation. One that is absolutely new
since the world began. Until now each human being,

from the time he was born, had to live with death —
with his death—as an imminent prospect. Now it is
the entire human species that survives, with the end
of the world (four or five buttons) as an imminent
prospect. The scientist immediately looks for an alibi,
which merely makes his responsibility stand out more
clearly. "If mankind disappears all at once, it will be a
case of suicide," he says. What murderer doesn't try
to camouflage his murder as suicide?

The strange part is that science and scientists still
have such prestige with other men! No one dares to
challenge them. So mankind remains faithful to the
most ancient kind of idolatry. It is the most cruel
sects which practiced idolatry most fanatically. The
idols which exacted the greatest number of human
sacrifices were the most passionately adored.

No matter! Whatever the secondary causes may be,
the Christian must always be ready: everyone must
die! And I have always known too, because I learned
it in catechism, that the world will end one day. Why
not today, or tomorrow? As De Gaulle retorted to
the Russian ambassador, who was brandishing the
threat of nuclear warfare, "In that case, Sir, we will
die together!" The main thing is not to be intimi-
dated. If the end of the world is to come, then let it
come! All of this is a reminder, on a planetary scale,
of what the ultimate outcomes will be, whether for an
individual or for the whole species: Death, Judgment,
Paradise or Hell. Until now we had been used to
saying that we had plenty of time and that anyhow
we would run into those ultimate outcomes only one
at a time, the way you go through a revolving door.

But now it seems that because of a slight pressure on four or five buttons, the entire human race will suddenly be transported to the other shore, at the feet of that King of Terror the Scriptures mention: *Dies irae, dies illa . . .*

As a sort of figment of the imagination, I suggested a Nuremberg trial for the ideas that have brought the world to where it is now. Nothing is harder—heroic, in a certain sense—than to subpoena the ideas we live on from day to day. It's as if we were being skinned alive. For instance, we might begin by making fun of scientists the way we make fun of professional soldiers. A Nobel Prize winner might, to our eyes, wear a uniform as suspect as that of a field marshal; for after all it's not because a man has won a Nobel Prize in physics, chemistry or medicine that he is infallible in every field and has the right to talk nonsense about man and his destiny. What am I saying! Scientists are a sacred and sacerdotal caste; they may do anything they like. If the holocaust of mankind comes to pass, it is they who will be its Grand Priests. And up to the very last minute we will go on hugging their knees.

But there is always another culprit whom we single out, in our everyday conversation, as the target of our vengeance, if not our justice, and sometimes even the

butt of our mockery. The culprit is God! How often
do we hear it said, and by people who are far from
stupid, "If there were a God, how could He have
allowed the atrocities we have seen? When you think
of all the misery that falls on innocent people, the
only excuse God can have is that He doesn't exist
. . ." These are not blasphemous questions; they genuinely arise. But interrogation leads too quickly to a
judgment which is worse than a sentence, a declara-
tion of non-existence. Which is also one more alibi. If
God does not exist, that does not eliminate death,
but it does eliminate the other ultimate outcomes:
Judgment, Paradise, Hell.

The negation spreads, step by step. Once it has
been decided that God is dead, why stop while the
going is so good? Now it is man himself who is being
denied, his essential distinctiveness, his unique language. Technology turns into hate. Technology
fashions a terribly effective instrument for imple-
menting the negations, the hate. We are not even
taken aback by the pitiless utterances of Dr. Barnard
when he proclaims that the problems involved in
heart surgery should be solved from a "medical"
viewpoint only, leaving aside all moral or religious
considerations. Above the patient's interest, above
the doctor's own interest, there is the higher interest
of medicine. The Hippocratic oath is more and more
neglected. Man today is no more than a guinea pig.

The truth is that within the development of modern society we cannot see any way of halting a
process which, having begun by eliminating God, is
now matter-of-factly going about the business of

eliminating the sacred distinctiveness of man. Sacred? Why should man be considered any more sacred than a guinea pig, after all? or a lobster? or a pebble? In a certain context of generalized, practical atheism, moral awareness itself looks like a very useless vestigial organ, which you can have amputated, in the name of preventive medicine, the way you can have your appendix removed.

I t is not in the Western countries but else-where that one gets a feeling of trudging slowly toward the light, of a determined effort being made to move through orthodoxies and emerge into truth, like a butterfly struggling to come out of its cocoon. The recent writers' trials in Russia are very meaningful here. The words which Ginzburg the poet spoke to his judges go very very far: "I will always be ready to die for my country but I cannot lie for it!" These are a martyr's words. They could be the reply of a Christian martyr—Christian according to the Gospel. They are certainly not the words of a Machiavelli or a Lenin.

Dying, lying! So difficult and so easy to die! Impossible to lie! Those are the boundaries of the lists in which honor is won, and doubtless grace as well. And all of this in connection with a country which is your homeland—how could there be a shorter way of

saying that the individual conscience transcends political obligation, that there is something in man which
dominates society; that this something which dominates society also transcends life and death, since men
are willing to die in order to preserve that integrity
and refuse to live if life is to be preserved at the
expense of it? Yes, these are indeed the essential features of martyrdom: death, to bear witness to what
exceeds life, to place its seal on what death cannot
touch.

What is that "something"? Let those who are sensitive to the moral dilemma which the young Russian
writer expressed so well—"Die, yes! Lie, no!"—
look for that something in themselves. They have it;
everyone has it; and that something begins to vibrate
like an echo at those valiant words of Ginzburg the
poet. Let's stay within earshot of this salutary
andante.

When you have seen a number of people die all
around you, especially when you have been privileged
to see them die in a great surge of life offered and
death accepted, then you know that there is something in man which goes beyond man—for after all,
why would I accept my own destruction if not in
order to save something in me which death cannot
destroy but which a single act—that of lying, for
example—could erase? Of course there are different
kinds of death. There are cowardly suicides, which
are lies to oneself and to everything. I am talking
about something else, with which I am familiar because I have witnessed it several times.

I might take as an example the execution of seven

young Communists, shot at Clairvaux prison on Ascension Day in 1942. Even in front of the firing
squad they sang the *Marseillaise* and the *Interna-
tionale:* "Ni Dieu ni César ni tribun!" They believed
they were atheists. They believed perhaps that their
destiny came to an end in that little cemetery; they
were singing. In the name of what? to save what? did
they so generously accept death? For France? For a
certain conception of freedom? So that their children, or their younger brothers—they were very
young themselves—would not live under tyranny?
Then their love of France, or of freedom, or of their
young brothers, was worth more to them than their
lives. Or perhaps out of sheer defiance?—for the sake
of saying *no,* and underscoring that *no* with their
blood. And yet if one had to choose between the
victims, who die, and the executioners, who survive,
who would not be on the victims' side? Why? In the
name of what? The fact is that I can never think back
to that execution without the image which I retain of
those seven young men being haloed by victory.
There can be no doubt that this execution, like so
many others, and this blood that was spilled, were an
affirmation in death of a reality which transcends
both life and death but which would have been de-
stroyed if those young men had denied it and betrayed it by going over to the enemy.

We ought to know by now that we are not beyond good and evil. Besides, what lies beyond good and evil actually lies, not beyond, but beneath. Good and evil are like gardening. A gardener who cared no more about flowers than about weeds would abandon his garden to grow wild. When someone claims to be beyond good and evil, he falls lower than the beasts, and barbarism carries the day. These obvious truths can be obscured and complicated by all kinds of philosophical considerations, but that does not alter the basic issue at stake. Of course words may be freely defined. But why challenge traditional definitions without some reason? The only reason Ginzburg refuses to lie is that lying is evil and that what seems to be the interest of his country cannot compensate for that evil. I say "seems" because in this instance, it is not Ginzburg but instead his judges who wrong the Russian fatherland. There are other ways of explaining this, using different words, but what it boils down to is that and nothing else.

But then what is this *good*, this business of not lying, which is placed even above the interest of the country, which one man takes it on himself to judge, since he refuses to sacrifice it to the demands of his judges? If we agree that there is a hierarchy of types of good among which one not only can but must choose, then we move away from physics and begin to engage in metaphysics. You take Russia, which has a physical weight, and you take judges who have a physical weight, since they can send you to prison, and above these you place a thing which no one can see, no one can grasp in his hands, which remains intact even in prison, even under the executioner's ax, which we can call honor, a sort of spiritual — that is, metaphysical—integrity. Ginzburg is engaged in metaphysics, certainly not in Marxism-Leninism. Now, as soon as you cross the threshold of metaphysics—no matter what you call it, or even if you don't call it anything at all—you move forward in the shadow cast by God.

Everyone knows the scene in the Gospel wherein man's relationships with God on the one hand, and with politics on the other, are defined. Everyone knows it and yet it continues to be scrutinized. Christ's enemies, who are formidable opponents, ask Him whether tribute should be paid to Caesar. A dangerous question in an occupied country which finds Caesar's sovereignty hard to bear. If Jesus answers that the tax should be paid, He will appear as a collaborator with the occupying power. If He answers that the tax should not be paid to Caesar, He will leave Himself open to a political accusation by the Roman authorities.

We know what Jesus answers. His answer may seem to be a clever one, since it springs the trap without His falling into it, but it is much more than merely clever: it is a sort of geography of the temporal and spiritual orientations of man. Christ asks that they show Him a coin.

"Whose image is this?"

"Caesar's."

"Then render unto Caesar what belongs to Caesar,

and unto God, what belongs to God."

This scene has been interpreted in three ways. The Jacobins, whose tradition is perpetuated very legitimately in the militant atheism of Communism, say—they have actually said it—"Everything belongs to Caesar; man has no other obligation than the obligation to the earthly group to which he belongs. Whatever claims to transcend that obligation is an alibi and an opiate."

In Jerusalem, I discussed this scene with an eminent Israeli jurist, who said to me that Christ, who was a member of the resistance, relied on religion and on religion only to justify His resistance to Caesar. What He meant was, "Everything belongs to God, nothing to Caesar. Everything belongs to God, your gold, your own persons, your lives, your country. And even what seems to belong to Caesar belongs still more to God!" I found this interpretation equally excessive and dangerous, and I told the jurist so. "You are the Jacobin of God," I said to him.

For the obvious meaning, the one that naturally presents itself to you when you read this scene, is clear enough, and it is difficult to get around it. His opponents spoke to Christ of Caesar only; it is He who also spoke about God. The essential element in His reply is His affirmation of a duality and consequently of an undeniable ambiguity of human affairs. Man must meet two claims, of unequal importance as to urgency and dignity but each legitimate and each supreme in its own order: the claim of Caesar and the claim of God. Caesar's demand is imperious; it goes so far as to demand that one die for him, as Ginzburg realized: "I am ready to die for my country," he said. But God's demand is superior, and also more universal and of a different order. It has to do with good and evil, with truth: "It is impossible for me to lie, even for my country." Except that Ginzburg does not talk about God. It is I who talk about Him.

When Christ came before His judge, Pontius Pilate, He said to him, "Yes, I am King, but my Kingdom is not of this world. I was born and I came into this world only for one thing: to bear witness to the truth." Then He added, "Everyone that is of the truth heareth my voice!" To which Pilate eternally answers, "What does one lie more or less matter, and anyhow what is truth?"

Obviously the men who judged Ginzburg — who is rotting away in a Russian prison right now for having refused to lie—those judges descend directly from Pilate. But what side is Ginzburg himself on? What voice did he hear? If it is true that Christ speaks to those who love truth, did He speak to Ginzburg? Where? How? Through what secret vibrations of the heart?

For that matter, how could we imagine even for one minute that Ginzburg is not a citizen of that Kingdom which, although it is not of this world, yet is in the world, and the characteristic of which is to shut out lies from within its borders, to welcome truth, to naturalize immediately all who love truth? Paying for belonging to the Kingdom of truth by going to prison for five years—which one of us would do this as simply and as naturally as Ginzburg did? Once again I find confirmation of what I have seen a hundred times in the course of my life: the revelation of Jesus Christ, of His teaching, of His person is infinitely more accessible, more concrete than the revelation of God; or rather, there is no true God except in Jesus Christ.

We must never tire of noting the importance of what Christ recognized: the presence of dual authorities, God and Caesar. Here is where we can, and must, speak of a double allegiance. I belong to God, body and soul; but I also belong to Caesar. To him too I belong body and soul, although with grave reservations especially where my soul is concerned. "Service to God first!" said Joan of Arc; yet until her very last sigh she demonstrated her second, and so very demanding, allegiance to her King and her country.

It is when men forget, or neglect, or deny one of these two allegiances that the worst kinds of perverseness, the worst catastrophes come to pass. When men recognize and proclaim only their allegiance to Caesar, to the exclusion of God, then we have the totalitarian state which is, logically enough, atheist. When men recognize and proclaim only their allegiance to God, even in earthly matters, then we have a theocracy. The Catholic Church is in the second category but its mission transcends this world, since that mission is to bear our souls up to the eternal life. If we are talking about a temporal republic which acknowledges only the authority of God even in temporal matters, then the door is left open to all types of fanaticism, as in the Florence of Savonarola's day, or in the Crusade of Mr. General Franco. This is another version of totalitarianism, and it is even more despicable than secular totalitarianism. The latter tyrannizes men in the name of Caesar only. To tyrannize them in the name of the true God is a blasphemy as well.

There is nothing easier for a man — because of laziness, or ambition, or lassitude, or stupidity, or cowardice, or a cynical taste for absolute power, or a desire to be adored — than to dream of a single allegiance, one, absolute, totalizing, and to be loyal to it, body and soul, forever. The history of mankind is filled with the ravages wrought by this simplifying dream, which eliminates one allegiance or the other, ultimately divinizing Caesar or Caesar-izing God and doing the greatest harm to man and society, to the worship due to the true God and the honest service due to Caesar.

I maintain that this frightful monism of allegiance is a permanent temptation in men's way and a poison lurking within all societies. "Sacralism" is not characteristic of the Middle Ages only; and besides, even in the Middle Ages, the Kings of France, at least, obstinately maintained the autonomy of the temporal power in relation to the spiritual power of the Pope and the bishops. Saint Louis (Louis IX) did this more than any other king. And that is the truth.

Having said this much, we must also say that even when they do not go to the extreme of claiming that all belongs to God and nothing to Caesar, even so all clerical men in all religions and in all eras are tempted to make abusive use of their spiritual authority for temporal purposes and to Caesarize God. All politicians in all eras, even if they do not assert that all belongs to Caesar and nothing to God, are tempted to extend their authority to the spiritual realm.

When Jean Giono, the writer, penned an introduction to a French edition of the complete works of Machiavelli, he began, with that gravity which ill-bred pedants always display, "The Rennaissance tried to see things as they were, no longer viewing them through the Christian illusion." If it weren't that we have long grown accustomed to putting up with everything, and that our critical spirit is worn right down to the bone, those words would make us break out immediately in loud guffaws. Where is the illusion? Where is lucidity? Doubtless the four centuries that separate us from Machiavelli have been filled with sound and fury. Machiavelli himself perpetuated a very ancient tradition which held that politics was an essentially cynical business and was limited to the art of conquering, keeping, exercising and extending power with no other limit than that of one force halted by another, greater force.

By the way, I am astonished to see how people have made Machiavelli into a thinker and a master. He was an observer of manners, and I do not think that his moral statements were meant as an example but as an expression of what he noted, as was the case with La Fontaine. The *Fables* of La Fontaine are the Machiavelli of the French. They are largely responsible for the way the modern French have settled into mediocrity. The fact that the *Fables* are ostensibly about animals does not make them innocuous.

For four centuries, Machiavelli has had disciple upon disciple. The Renaissance Princes, including the Popes, followed his advice and gloried in their deceitfulness. Frederic II, Napoleon Bonaparte, Bismarck, Cavour were good pupils of Machiavelli. German philosophy clothed his observations with the dignity of intellectual necessity. Modern revolutions have been launched according to the same rules. If you reread Lenin, Trotsky or Hitler, you find that nothing in their strategy or their tactics contradicts Machiavelli, but that everything, on the contrary, contradicts "the Christian illusion." In the last analysis, all of this fine politicking, heroic and lucid although it was supposed to be, ended in catastrophes, in which life and honor and human dignity were squandered and tossed to all the winds of History.

Why not? On the face of it, and solely from the standpoint of power to be conquered and exercised, there is no reason why men should not be treated as passive instruments, mere pawns on a chessboard.

Why should they be considered any more valuable than that? When you come right down to it—and this is an unavoidable conclusion to be drawn—shoving men into a crematory oven is no more important than plunging live lobsters into boiling water. Is that what is meant by striving to see the world as it is, quite aside from "the Christian illusion"? That seems to me more like a diabolical act of cheating, a shameful, cruel masquerade of essential, inalienable reality. I refuse to concede that this kind of conduct has the merit of being lucid, and still less of being heroic.

I call to witness all who, throughout the long combat which my generation fought, saw others all around them die a violent death, in a spirit of lucidity and acceptance, in concentration camps or cells or before firing squads. In circumstances like those, it is the world such as it is which is the illusion and the world beyond this world which suddenly becomes reality of the most urgent sort. It can even happen— and I saw it several times—that people are willing to die joyously, to see the world such as it is erased with a wave of the hand. At times like that, the man who is going to die refuses to lie; it doesn't occur to him to lie. It is the man who is going to die who is free. Free, and free of illusion.

The truth is that man is either sacred—i.e., that

with one part of his being he belongs to an untouch-
able universe—or else he is entirely enclosed in nature,
and his fate is no more important than the fate of
lobsters. Now, we are willing to subscribe to a
philosophy that puts man on the same level as the
lobster. Furthermore, we agree that it is all right to
throw lobsters into boiling water; but we are not
willing—not yet, at least—to agree that it is all right to
shove children into a crematory oven.

Modern intelligence is pharisaical. It refuses to
criticize its philosophy but at the same time it also
refuses the practical consequences of that philosophy.
I must admit that if I myself, who am a simple man
and probably a very crude one, were so unfortunate
as to believe sincerely in a materialistic philosophy,
which reduces man to a phenomenon, a social creature, a quirk of chance; if I were to believe that, then
I would go all the way, and the Nazis' crimes would
seem perfectly normal to me; in other words, they
would not be crimes to me. If you insist that man be
given special treatment, then first of all you must
recognize his distinctiveness.

But we hate distinctiveness. From the outset, before we have stopped to think about it, we hate it.
How could we discover it? How could we respect it?
How could we love it enough to shed all the blood of
the body, so necessary in order to proclaim that this
difference exists and that it is inviolable, sacred? We
Christians say that man is created in God's image and
that this is what makes him distinct from the whole
material universe, what gives him his sacred role, his
highest allegiance. Created in God's image, he belongs

to God first of all. It is this allegiance loftier than the
world that is the source of his independence with
respect to everything, absolutely everything that is
not God. God is the master of disillusion with respect
to all that is not Himself.

Why? Because God is distinction itself in every
sense of the word. He is the infinitely separated; His
difference is absolute; one can never resemble Him
other than very remotely and by analogy. In speaking
of Him, it is always more affirmative, more suitable,
more expressive to use "no" than to use "yes."

When our horrible modern demagogues of theology
come and explain to us in alluring tones that God is
dead, they are not even saying the same thing as
Nietszche did. Nietszche wanted to set man free and
place him at the pinnacle of the universe, asserting his
supreme and independent distinction. Today, when
we are told that God is dead, this is a demagogic set
phrase expressing the hatred of any kind of distinction. It is also the first step toward the negation
of man, a statement that man himself is reduced and
defined entirely within the banal categories and structures of matter. Man is no longer distinct in any way,
not even as one head of cattle among the herd; he is
mass-produced like an assembly-line automobile, all
of whose parts, both psychic and physical, are inter-
changeable.

We will move closer and closer to a totalitarianism
that will reduce everything to the same level, to a
robotized mankind. Either that, or else we will have
to hoist the flag and do battle to restore all distinctions at the same time.

It is strange to think that it is behind the Iron Curtain that the first indications have appeared that intelligence may eventually resume its ancient function of non-conformity, of doubting, questioning, of refusing ready-made rules, of putting up resistance to a monolithic type of justice—in other words, its sovereign function of guiding, wisely discerning, distinguishing: dying is one thing, lying is another. To die freely for one's country is to take a solemn oath of allegiance to a Kingdom which is supreme in this world. To lie would be to deny a sacred allegiance to another Kingdom which is also supreme but which is in another world, beyond this one. Two Kingdoms, God and Caesar, God and politics. The modern monism—a single allegiance that devours man whole and that was also the allegiance of the most antique paganism, the most barbarous paganism, when each people walked with its own god, which was not its neighbor's god — this monism is beginning to crack and crumble; and in the depths of a Russian prison, we are coming back, slowly, to the distinction between God and Caesar which the Christ made one day when a hand held out a gold coin to Him.

Once again, Ginzburg did not talk about God; at least, he did not mention the word God. He is a communist; he was born and grew up in a State which is officially atheist. In the open conflict which he had with his country's judges, he merely refused them what they were demanding: a lie; nothing but a lie. But in the name of what, or of whom, did he refuse?

In any case, this means that the State and its justice do not have all the rights, and that not everything in man belongs to the State. What is this part of man which does not belong to the State? It is called the conscience. But if Ginzburg's conscience forbids him to lie ("I cannot"), then it transcends Ginzburg himself; it enacts the will of a judge superior to those on earth. It is this invisible Judge of men's consciences that we call God.

So, one can appeal, as Ginzburg did, from the judges of this earth to that other judge, of whom the individual conscience is at once the mediator and the expression. But even for Ginzburg, there can be no higher appeal than to conscience. Man's conscience opens from the top and confides in a supreme court of justice, which is a mystery but whose voice is irrefutable. "Everyone that is of the truth heareth my voice." We can clearly see that man's conscience transcends the tribunals of this world only because it reflects in this world a judiciary which is not of this world.

This fully corresponds to what we Christians know: that man is created in God's image and is meant to dominate this world. What I am submitting here is not a demonstration of the Judeo-Christian revelation—there is no adequate demonstration of the divine revelation; but this inherent distinction, one conscience becoming two in order to face two duties, two orders, two different worlds, this decisive fissure introduced into the social monism (which may be natural to us, the way it is to bees and ants) is the admirable illustration of the lesson (and it is precisely a supernatural one) taught by Genesis, as well as by the Gospel.

Russia, the Russia of Ivan the Terrible just like Stalin's Russia, has always followed in the footsteps of Byzantium. It is the fatherland of Caesaro-papism, which Caesarized God. Communist Russia has reversed the situation: now it is Caesar who is divinized. It remains a monist political regime and, to my way of thinking, an essentially sacral, though atheistic, one. In either case, the political authority remains supreme and it is the sole authority; either the Czar, who is already consecrated the temporal head, is also head of the Church; or the political power, by making atheism the State religion, claims all authority for itself.

Ginzburg came to know this firsthand. His trial was essentially an Inquisition trial. His judges did not in the least appreciate the distinction he made between dying and lying. By making that distinction, he defied the sacral monism. He had it coming: off to jail! But Ginzburg's exemplary case was like the one swallow which, although it may not make a summer, or even a spring, does at least herald its coming. The thaw will begin; the iceberg has cracked; it is about to crumble.

The day that fissure has widened under the pressure of the most profound demands of the conscience, and the State is forced to recognize a realm of conscience which transcends it, the day the State is judged according to an authority superior to its own, that day, Russian youth will discover with delight, with all of the religious ardor of which it is still capable—Holy Mother Russia cannot be made to disappear!—that, above the allegiance to Caesar, there is another human allegiance, from which man draws his freedom. One cannot be veritably free except through a superior allegiance.

A good beginning has been made! Perhaps it was necessary to go through the sacral monism of atheism in order to discover the need to distinguish between the two cities. The day that the younger Russian generation discovers—as Ginzburg has done—that one can pass judgment on one's masters, it is not at all certain that it will revert to a Byzantine regime of Caesaro-papism, nor should it. That is the past, buried once and for all. What is to be ardently hoped for is that Russian youth will definitively turn its back on any form of sacral monism, whether religious or atheistic, and that it will savor the liberation to be found in its double allegiance, rendering of course unto Caesar what belongs to Caesar but rendering also unto God what belongs to God. Then that great people will arise and will be ready to embark, with its eyes open, on the twofold adventure of civil liberty and spiritual liberty.

Part 2

The Church and the Revolution

O ne of Jacques-Bénigne Bossuet's orations begins in these now-classic terms: "He who reigns in heaven and on whom all empires depend ..." Here we are at the heart of the matter. So, God has to do with empires, and with the government of men constituted in a society?

For a long time, probably for thousands and thousands of years, the question was never even raised; it just went without saying. Each nation walked with its gods; the chief of the clan was patriarch, pontiff and king all at the same time; over every member of his clan he had the right of life or death, the right of pardon. For each clan, religion occupied the place of politics; the clan's victories and defeats were the victories and defeats of its gods. It is not pointless in our day to review this primitive clan structure, which Aristotle in his own day already found barbaric, for there is nothing to prove that the present social trend is not bringing us slowly back to that barbarous state. When divine attributes are conferred upon a State, it is politics which ends up taking the place of religion, just as eternity is dissolved in history. What an extraordinary paradox to pin the label of "progress" on what is actually a fearsome regression!

This is probably where the most deep-seated identity between national-socialism and communism is to be found: both confer a divine character upon History, and both, seeing no finality for man except in time, make politics absolute, actually idolatrous, endowing it in fact with all the qualifications which Marx grants religion—and first among them, the quality of being, to an exceptional degree, an opiate.

The destiny of Israel is altogether separate, altogether unique. This people too, like all the other clans, walked with its God. Only, this is the thing: its God was absolutely unlike the other gods. All the other gods were false gods. Only the God of Israel was the true God.

Without knowing the context we cannot evaluate how insolent, peremptory and revolutionary such a pretention was. In a completely idolatrous world, only this stiff-necked little people was right. The people of Israel spent their time rhapsodizing about the virtues and the splendid deeds of their God. It was Israel's God who had brought heaven and earth out of nothingness, who had created the constellations in the sky and all the fishes of the sea; He had made man in His own image; He probed loins and hearts. He was the master of history, the universal judge.

In an age when the dignity of a god was measured by the mightiness of the nation he protected, Israel reversed the relationship. Its God was the all-mighty par excellence; having created the world and all the peoples that dwelt in it, He rightfully held universal sway. Instead of the people proving the power of its God, it was God who would ensure the glory of Israel. From its inception, then, monotheism was identified with the ambition of conquering and dominating the universe. What could be more logical? If one people among all the peoples, no matter how small it may be, has for its God the only true God, the creator of the universe, it is only normal that one day that people should receive, as a heritage, the whole of heaven and all the earth. It was certainly the true God who put such ideas into the Jews' heads.

Then come the Prophets. They do not alter the universality of the Promise made to the descendants of Abraham. They simply try to say that that heritage must be construed in a more spiritual than political way. But it is not until the advent, within Judaism itself, of Jesus Christ and His message that one can be altogether certain that the Promise made to Abraham will be fulfilled on the spiritual plane, in the universal Church, and hereafter, in eternal Paradise, and that any member whosoever of the human species can be grafted, by baptism and faith, onto the authentic trunk of the stock of Abraham.

Everything fits together. Until a much later period in their history, the Jews of the Old Testament scarcely believed in the eternal life, the hereafter. So, for them, God's Promise could have only a temporal meaning, of immediate fulfillment in this world, for them or their descendants. Hence, the paradox by which this little people, solely because of its monotheism, sincerely believed that it was elected to dominate the universe. On several occasions, in fact, this political ambition came close to being realized. Perhaps it was in Christ's own day that the climate was most favorable to its realization, what with the diffusion of Jewish thought through Philo Judaeus of Alexandria, the international scope of Jewish trade, fostered by the Pax Romana, and the amorous maneuvers of Jewish women, the most famous of whom is still Berenice.

Christ put a halt to that ambition and stripped it of all legitimacy, and that is probably what His own nation could not forgive Him for. By asserting that the Kingdom of God, while of this world, stretched beyond this world and could be attained only hereafter, and by recognizing too that Caesar had a legitimate share in the affairs of this world, He was of course purifying the antique religion of Israel, but He was also, once and for all, setting aside all nationalism and all political maneuvers. Moreover, within Judaism itself, the resurrection of Christ, when He broke into eternal life, body and soul, the way a burglar breaks into a house, shattered all existing conventions. After Him, it was impossible to be unaware that the Promise of universal domination made to Abraham and his seed must be taken in the sense of a spiritual catholicity, consummated in eternity. In other words, Christianity stood revealed as the spiritual and fully religious interpretation, the heroic aspiration, of all Judaism.

Contrariwise, within Christianity itself, there is a permanent temptation to regress toward the Old Testament, to what has, historically, been most materialistic and most temporal about it. The temptation is especially strong today, when the prestige of science, the achievements of technology, the most modern theories on the nature of man and the universe place the preoccupation with the historical record, with instant success, with clear and seemingly irrefutable explanations in a much more compelling light than the hope of eternal life. People believe in the coming of the universal Kingdom of reconciliation—but through the great, fashionable ideologies: Freudianism or Marxism. People are still willing to accept Christ—but as the God-Man to come, the omega of evolutionary trends.

In which case, and no matter what ideologies are used to camouflage the fact, it is normal—it is logical

—it is inevitable that Christianity should lose its orientation toward the hereafter and the eternal, that it should become confused with a certain type of politics—in short, that it should become a vulgar, earthly Messianism, flatly contradicting the Gospel of Jesus Christ, contradicting the Passion, the death and the resurrection of that same Jesus Christ. The miraculous thing about it is that this contradiction is not obvious to everyone.

When I talk in these terms, I believe that I am, unfortunately, telling the truth. In the defamation campaign launched against the Church and its past—which some people hold to be blameworthy at every stage in its history since Constantine—I see an attempt to use spiritual matter to temporal ends and, more specifically, to modify the organization of the Church for purposes of political conquest and power. Some people, I say, are determined not to miss the boat this time toward mastery of the world.

These people feel that once the vast machinery of the Catholic Church, which does in fact cover the entire planet, has been tinkered with, once "reliable" or at least pliable leaders have been placed at the positions of command, it will be a vehicle with many flaws but which, if properly driven, can conduct them to that universal domination of hearts and minds that they so passionately desire. To their way of thinking, no matter how effectively sociology, psychology, Freudianism and the various Marxisms may "explain" human nature, i.e., dominate it in order to recreate man in the image of a dream yet to come, they still need that extra something, soul, which only Christianity can give them.

"We feel that we are in a strong position," they say. "We will deal as one power to another. We laugh at those who accuse us of betraying the Church when we are certain that, on the contrary, we are actually saving it from what would otherwise have been its fate: ending up in an antiques museum. We and we alone are offering a future to that old Church, we alone assign it a place of honor in the modern world. We are putting a new engine into that old chassis, we are taking all the risks on its behalf. Thanks to us, the Church can begin to move again, pick up the infallible rhythm of progress, climb onto the bandwagon of the future. What is more, we are determined to win, determined not to let anyone get the better of us. We've made up our minds to get a good price for that extra dose of soul that we have to offer and the modern world so sorely needs. We will not trade it for anything less than a share in the ranks of power that govern the planet. 'You shall sit upon thrones, judging the twelve tribes!' After all, that promise too is found in the Gospels!"

This is the way they talk. These are men of the Old Testament, using the language and displaying the impatience of the Old Testament. This is also the language of the Apostles, until the morning of the Ascension: "Lord, has the time come at last when You will seize the throne of Israel?" This is irritating language; it grates on the ear. Must we be patient with those who are so lacking in patience? Yet Jesus' answer is disconcertingly, inflexibly gentle: "It is not given to you to know the days and the hours which my Father, in His might, has set aside."

When you come right down to it, the opportunistic little demagogues of theology are not so stupid when they hammer away, inside the edifice of Christianity, at the image of the Father; for it is the mightiness of the Father which stands in the way of their immediate ambitions. Isn't it marvelous! Here they are obsessed with the temporal element to the exclusion of all else, claiming to be the supreme omens of that element (days and hours), impatient to decipher the signs of it so as to take advantage of them, make them an algebraic equation of success—and then Christ gently warns them that it will never be possible for them who are His Apostles, to decipher those signs, for the key to them lies hidden at the bottom of a well of eternity.

And then the Christ promises that the Holy Spirit will descend and He issues His supreme commandment: "Be my witnesses!", to the very ends of the earth and of time. Witnesses: the whole truth, nothing but the truth, nothing more nor less, nothing else; raise your hand and repeat, "I swear it." Yes, we have sworn to transmit this Gospel truth, never diminishing it, not overburdening it either.

Then Christ is taken away up into heaven; a cloud hides Him from their sight. And there we stand, between Ascension and Pentecost, with our noses in the air as we gaze up into the sky. The Christ was taken away from us; He is well hidden from our sight. And we do not yet have the strength and the consolation of the Holy Spirit.

After all, men are free. God made them that way a long time ago. For a long time the Devil too has been telling them so: "You shall be like gods, knowing good and evil." If the men of today forget the eternal dimension of Christianity, which is what makes it so precious, and are absolutely bent on reverting to the Old Testament, that's their own business. But God too is free. He may very well end up dealing with us as He did with the men of the Old Testament, by meting out immediate rewards and immediate punishment.

The ten plagues of Egypt offer a striking analogy with what we call environmental pollution today: "The fish that were in the river died, and the river stank, and the Egyptians could not drink of its waters." Enlightened as we are of course by the revelations of science and the wonders of technology, we will steadfastly refuse to see in this the workings of God. Our intelligence is so short-sighted that secondary causes are all we need. We must be like Pharaoh, whose heart grew harder with each plague that ravaged his country. Today Pharaoh would be a Nobel Prize-winning scientist and he would explain it all in down-to-earth terms. His explanations would leave us gaping but just as helpless as before when the next plague came along.

I am a man of queries and hypotheses. I belong to an intellectual tradition—the Dominican tradition—which does not fear any question, which functions only through questions. I insist—it is my right to insist—that my partner in dialogue maintain the same openness of mind. Regardless of what my personal convictions may be, I am not afraid to ask myself, fully, whether God exists. Obviously, if God does not exist, many things become pointless, beginning with this very book. But why would even an adamant non-believer refuse to consider the hypothesis that God exists, God the creator of heaven and earth, the beatific finality of man, the supreme judge of the spirit?

And so, no matter what the immediate reasons, the natural, measurable, observable, scientific, technical reasons for so destructive a phenomenon as pollution, why shouldn't we grope beyond those reasons and onto a metaphysical level? Why shouldn't we have the premonition that what we are actually seeing in the pollution of nature, alongside and in addition to all those reasons, is the reflection of a divine punitive intention? Chance and necessity, on the level of phenomena, absolutely do not rule out a hereafter of those same phenomena, scene of action of another causality, supreme this time, which would not overlap the immediate causalities but would contain them all to the highest degree, a causality that would be both free and necessary at the same time but not absurd. The modern world makes a Promethean effort to do without God, to eliminate all authentic religion. Well! the result may not be as beneficial as had been hoped. A world without God doesn't seem to be working so very well.

I've been talking about God. We might talk about the Devil as well, at least insofar as a certain more concentrated, more virulent form of stupidity is the mark of the Devil, who likes to ape God and only manages to make faces. When I say this I have in mind the pollution of nature. Just at the time when peoples all over the world are beginning to grow deeply anxious about pollution, just then is when the priests stop the Rogation Days processions in which, every spring, the Church used to seek God's blessing on the trees and the animals, the fields and the waters, the vines and the grain, the fishes and the birds.

The French government has recently given us a Secretary of the Environment. But it is not up to him, after all, to go chanting the litanies of the saints while sprinkling the meadows and the woods with holy water. The priests no longer believe in what they should be doing, because they no longer want to live up to their vocation, which is concerned with things sacred. Now of course it is not so easy as it used to be to conduct a Rogations procession, what with today's automobile traffic and police regulations. But why not modernize the procession, which is more necessary than ever before? Personally, I don't see why Rogations should not be conducted by helicopter; the bishop could wear his miter, hold the crosier in his left hand and the aspergillum in his right, and the helicopter would carry him through the sky to bless what used to be that garden beloved of God— France. And a huge radio set would send out over the air the litanies of the saints, that garland of the Church triumphant.

If God is the creator of heaven and earth, He might just have some ideas on the pollution of nature. We might just beseech Him from time to time not to let that creation which He made so beautiful and helpful in the beginning become foul and defaced.

W as there ever a time that abounded so in miracles?

But these are inside-out miracles, things one would never even have thought possible, so dazzling is their stupidity, and they pour down upon all of us until we are dazed and bewildered, unable to utter a sound or formulate a criticism. There ought to be a continuous contest. In the old days, the priest, high up in his pulpit, used to single out a child from among the parishioners and have him recite a catechism lesson during the service. Now I propose that in just the same way, the priest up in that same pulpit should tell his flock, now and again, about the most monumental idiocy recently committed by a liturgist or a demagogue of theology or simply an historian. It would not take long to compile an incomparable collection of nonsense. It would certainly be our turn to make fun of the Devil, and it seems to me that the churches would be appropriate places for taking this innocent revenge on the absurdity of our day.

The other evening, on one of the larger private radio stations, I heard an uppity female with a smattering of theology explain to us in a voice that was

meant to be solemn that the Catholic Church, from
the time of Constantine the Great right down to
Cardinal Marty today—for it was actually about him
that she was talking—had lived in a state of submis-
siveness vis-a-vis political authority and had been un-
worthy of its vocation of justice and brotherhood.
According to this little hussy, it was not until just
lately that the Church became adult and had the
courage to take on its true mission and display the
lofty independence of its vocation.

Now, whom is she taking us for? With all my heart,
I wish the bishops of our day had the stature, the
lucidity, the courage of so many bishops in the past
with respect to the civil authorities. One can only
hope that they will find the strength of an Athanasius
confronting the Arian emperors, or of an Ambrose
confronting a Theodosius the Great, of a Gregory VII
confronting the emperor Henry IV, even of a Fénelon
opposing Louis XIV, or a Pius VII confronting
Napoleon I. The mission of our Church is in fact to
produce saints in the image of Our Lord Jesus Christ,
who valiantly defied the national authorities and did
not back down before Caesar's representative, the
Procurator Pontius Pilate. Never, from Constantine's
day to our own, has the Church ceased to produce
saints, whether big or little, obscure or famous. May
it keep on producing more — that is essentially what
is expected of it.

But paradoxically, what shows through all of these
silly charges is an enterprise which is similar to what
Constantine is reproached with. Just what is he reproached with? With the basest sort of moral compro-

mise in the interests of collusion between the Church and the temporal power. There can be no doubt that that reproach is well-founded. I know there is nothing pretty about seeing a party which has long been clandestine suddenly triumph in broad daylight. Immediately, no matter where it occurs, it is like a reward for spoils hunters. This is what happened when Constantine made Christianity the State religion: the cream of the young Christian generation in Rome was sickened by it and withdrew into the desert so as not to be an accomplice to the fact, a little like today's hippies fleeing the insolent metropolises. It was at this time that so many anchorites appeared and so many monasteries were founded in the deserts of upper Egypt.

Fine! But what's being readied for us today, underhandedly, is that same collusion between the Church and another temporal power, and it is no less guilty, no less dangerous. Only this time the temporal power which is preparing to lay its hand on the Church is not that of any Emperor or divine-right monarch; it is the ineffable power, supposedly of divine right as well, of the advancing Revolution. And there go our progressive little priests, climbing on each other's shoulders to wave as high in the sky as they can the labarum that will dazzle their Revolutionary brothers: *In hoc signo, vinces!* By this sign thou shalt vanquish!

The kind of Revolution they mean and to which they are asking us to rally is, like Constantine the Great, a temporal power, with its starting point in time: oppression of the working class by the middle class, and its culmination in time: the necessary and final triumph of the pure hard Revolution, here confused with the advent of the Kingdom of God, God being in fact nothing more than mankind reconciled with itself by the grace of almighty History.

So if there is anyone who has no right to raise his voice against Constantine, it is certainly our little revolutionary priests, who dream of nothing more nor less than another Caesaro-papism. Revolution will be no less hard a master for the Church than the worst of Emperors. And anyhow, in the field which is the Church's own home ground, at the junction of time and eternity, the Revolution will be just as abusive and just as illegitimate a master as the encroachments of any Caesar, no matter which one—not because it is the Revolution but because, like any other Caesar, it is an exclusively temporal power, yet would be trying to operate in an area which is completely out of its ken.

I dropped the word "Caesaro-papism." It's a big word, full of history, full to bursting. It's worth defining closely. A. A. Vasiliev, the eminent historian of Byzantium, quotes a late twelfth-century writer, Isaac the Angel, in this connection, and the words are so insolent that they take your breath away. Here is what that Byzantine writer had to say: "On earth, there is no distinction between the power of God and the power of the Emperor. Princes have the right to do anything they wish; and they may make use of what belongs to God just as of what belongs to themselves, without the slightest scruple. For it is from God that they received their investiture as emperors, and between God and themselves, there is no longer any difference."

Now, there is a clear and frankly horrifying text. It expresses the unreserved annexation of inalienable rights of God for the benefit of a political power which is merely human and temporal. When it reaches this point, Caesaro-papism is a form of idolatry. As always, Thomas Aquinas is incomparable in his definition of idolatry: "Among the gravest sins committed against God, by far the gravest is the sin by which a man grants to a creature the honor which is due to God. For by diminishing the princely authority of God, man, insofar as he is able to, constitutes unto himself and in this world, another god than God." Carried to its extreme, Caesaro-papism is just that: the fact of constituting unto oneself, in the affairs of this world, another god (the Emperor) than the true God.

The so-called "progressive" Christians are committing this same sin of idolatry. Only instead of adoring Caesar, who was very much a flesh-and-blood idol, they adore an idea, a utopia, the Revolution. Which does not make it any the less a shameful and detestable idolatry. No one will deny that a large part of the young clergy today is fascinated by the Revolution, and their fascination is of a mystical sort. In fact it is the mystical character of their fascination that serves as their alibi. They consider that God is the Revolution—God Himself at work within History.

During the Nazi occupation, the French bishops proclaimed that it was our duty to obey the aged Marshal Pétain, and that if we did not, we would be *committing a mortal sin*. In 1944, in my book entitled *Si grande Peine (One Sky to Share)*, I went so far as to lay a solemn question before those bishops: the Catholics who had taken part in the Resistance had not obeyed Pétain; by the same token, they had disobeyed their bishops' instructions and, according to those same instructions, had committed a mortal sin. Now, a mortal sin is a mortal sin; and one must confess it and repent of it in order to be pardoned. So, the question I raised in October 1944 was this: now that Pétain had been defeated, should the Catholics who had taken part in the Resistance and disobeyed him still accuse themselves of this mortal sin and repent of it, in order to be pardoned? Never did this solemn question, which was linked so closely to moral theology and the responsibilities of the French bishops, receive any answer. What conclusion is one to draw?

Our French Caesaro-papism which does not, of course, have the proud ostentation of the Byzantine tradition, has changed hats. But it is not by wearing the hat of Revolution, after having worn for so long the hat of established order, that our Caesaro-papism, changes its true nature. It remains what it always has been: a ferocious type of clericalism, aggravated by opportunism. One striking example was that good

Cardinal Suhard, who would have made an excellent Carthusian monk, but who was as well suited to being Archbishop of Paris as the Eiffel Tower is suited to bicycling around France. It was not until Paris was liberated, in August 1944, that he finally realized the errors of judgment and the moral compromises of which he had been guilty, right down to the very last minute of the Occupation. So, in order to clear himself, what did I see him do but give the heartiest welcome to the most suspect of the young resistance priests, the ones whose wartime camaraderie had made them lean sharply toward Marxism. Once you have acquired a taste for moral compromise, what difference does it make whether you compromise with the rightists or the leftists? But what we demand is a Church that does not compromise itself at all, a Church which is first and foremost, in all things, and above all things, the sole Bride of Christ.

In that passage from Isaac the Angel that I quoted above, all you have to do is replace the word "Emperor" with the word "Revolution," and there you have the ideal definition of Christian progressivism, which is the contemporary form of Caesaropapism: "On earth, there is no distinction between the power of God and the power of the Revolution. The leaders of the Revolution have the right to do anything they wish; and they may make use of what belongs to God just as of what belongs to themselves, without the slightest scruple. For it is from God that they received their investiture as leaders of the Revolution, and between God and themselves, there is no longer any difference." By nature, the idolatry of the

Revolution is identical to the idolatry of Caesar.

All I am trying to say is this: from the Christian point of view, unconditional devotion to the Revolution is no better than devotion to the Emperor. In both cases, the eternal is submerged in the historical; the Kingdom of God is bereft of that dimension of eternity, that inherent transcendency which are essential to it.

So, one cannot help but calmly contradict that charming woman we heard on the radio: Constantine the Great is not dead! On the contrary, he is more alive than ever before!

Surely, if there is one thing in the world to which I personally am sensitive, to say the least, one thing which fascinates me heart and soul and which could (I can feel it) spellbind me, it is the Marxist Messianism and Hegelianism. Once this attraction has been freed of all its intellectual trappings, which are rather mediocre after all, and it appears, ardent and naked, before the Christian conscience, it has a name: it is the impatience of hopefulness, the impatience which so easily turns into despair. My most violent temptations, the most dangerous ones, the ones that have nearly capsized my soul time and again are not temptations against faith but temptations against the second virtue, which is hope — the

temptations that appear amidst the dark reaches of
passions and violent desires, when one feels that the
Kingdom of God is growing more remote, that it is
retreating and drifting away, just as during a storm,
sometimes, you begin to believe that the sun will
never come back, never again, that it has fled forever
to the other side of the world.

"Aw, what's this business about waiting indef-
initely for the Kingdom of God without even knowing the days and the hours, and hoping for the return
of He who is to come back amid the heavenly hosts,
and keeping your ear cocked for the first notes from
the great trumpet, and going on doing it day after
day, and year after year and century after century —
it's too tiring, takes too much out of you. It's even
ambiguous. Maybe it's a trick, a hoax . . . And anyhow that kind of Kingdom is too high up, too far
away; as a matter of fact it's too good for the likes of
me. Why not go for a Kingdom on the human scale?
Why couldn't happiness come in this world, right
now?" Thus speak the voices of the earth! Thus spake
those voices one day to the heart of the Russian people, so profoundly Christian, so profoundly geared to
eschatology and the expectation of the afterlife,
which one day, through a sudden mutation, assigned
itself the task of creating and organizing the happiness of man here on earth. A painful dream, an impossible, inordinate dream, but it crucifies all the
same! A suffering people, a people of martyrs, a people that stands as witness to all that exceeds man, a
people that despaired of hope but did not deny the
cross for all that, did not toss it away in a ditch

along the long, long road, a people which will recommence to astound the world when once it suddenly begins to despair of the world and despair of its own despair!

The most timely parable is the parable of the Prodigal Son. The sin of the Prodigal Son is the sin against hope.

Balzac, who laid bare the deepest-lying motivations of our political history, wrote that in beheading King Louis XVI, the French people had cut off the head of every father of every family in France. I deeply believe that. I believe that the crisis afflicting family life in France is more than an ordinary stage in the economic and sociological development of our modern society. In France, it also has a much more disturbing, supernatural element. In fact Balzac could have added that in immolating the anointed King, the people actually wanted to kill God as well. The French people remain logical even when delirious. When you reread Saint-Just and the Marquis de Sade's famous pamphlet, you understand to just what an extent the murder of the King was a deliberately sacrilegious act, voluntarily profaning the coronation at Reims; it was the black mass of French history, and we have not yet experienced the ultimate consequences of it. It was a symbolic, theatrical act, suited to the genius of that people, and it dominates the history of France just as much as the baptism of Clovis at Reims in 496 or the sacrificial, triumphal adventure of Joan of Arc—but in the opposite way. It was not a profane society which dipped its seal in the blood of Louis XVI but, instead, a counter-

Christianity: by immolating the Lord's Anointed, this people, as a people, renounced its lofty hope of the Kingdom of God.

By that I do not mean to say that I regret the past. Some ruptures are irreparable, and you cannot set the clock back. The solution of contemporary problems does not lie behind but ahead of us. It is up to us to be the midwife of history, and our generations will be judged on the type of hope they will have left behind them. But in order to understand our age, it is just as well to trace back effects to their causes and discern in what way the consequences bear out or avenge the principles. Possibly, the ritual murder of the King was not the cause of anything at all; possibly it was just a flash bursting on the night, but what it reveals is unforgettable. It is the dazzling sign of a mysterious and terrible conflagration.

I f God has politics of some sort, He certainly hides the fact well. He never defines it, never posts it on the walls. It is not outlined by any statement, any manifesto, any platform. The Popes' muddled utterances in the realm of day-to-day politics merely throw their listeners off the track and definitely distract the attention of anyone seeking to espy the mysterious signs of a divine policy. We are at least very certain that God is not — could not be — a

politician. Not that He is aloof from what is called
politics; on the contrary, He is deeply involved in it,
just as a supreme finality is involved in the choice of
the means to attain it. How could God be unin-
terested in the story of mankind, of which He is the
final chapter? For if it is He who created man out of
the clay of the earth, then it is also He who is the
culmination of the human adventure. Like God,
Christ is obviously lord of all creation. But through
His redeeming grace as the Crucified and Resuscitated
Being, He is also and especially the king and the center of all hearts, the supreme hope of nations. He is
the hereafter of the evolution of peoples and of mankind. He is the grand Morning, which follows the
grand Evening of all revolutions. It is possible that
even before our generation is laid away under the
earth, this truth will become dazzlingly, terrifyingly
obvious to all. The peoples may be more weary than
one supposes of immediate horizons and the good
things of this world only.

One can only try to guess the way in which Jesus is
awaiting the return of the peoples to the fold, as the
shepherd awaits the return of his flock, at dusk. That
is what I mean when I say that the story of the Prodigal Son is the parable of modern times, which were
ushered in when the anointed King was put to death
and the political order was profaned.

When one sees what havoc is wreaked by ideologies, one might be tempted to hate them. But it
would be an error to scorn them. Even if they are
excessive and often false, they continue to be valuable as symptoms, from the clinical standpoint. For

instance, what are we to think of the vogue which, thanks to Freudianism, is now enjoyed by certain theories that exalt the murder of the Father, the fading away of the paternal Image, rebellion against the Father — theories that so many sociologists, not to mention the "in" young demagogues of theology are so full of. The Parable of the Prodigal Son begins, "Father, give me the portion of the inheritance that falls to me." What more certain way of moving up in the order of succession than by killing the Father? That is what the modern world has done, or at least what it intended to do when it abolished the image of the Father-King. If we cannot kill God, then we can at least eliminate Him from our society and consider Him as good as dead. Once the murder has been committed, ideology comes to the aid of the parricide to help him justify his crime—first of all in social terms, but in his own eyes most of all, for a criminal finds it excruciatingly unbearable to be fully, lucidly aware that he is a criminal.

It's at this point that I observe a clinical symptom in all of these eloquent or not-so-eloquent theories, that are intended to be shocking and scandalous, about the death of God and the disappearance of the Father and even of the Christian revelation, whereas Christianity is absolutely inconceivable without the Father, the first Person of the Holy Trinity. These theories do not really explain anything, but a certain remorse shows through them that has not been completely stifled, along with a certain cheap bragging which does not excuse the crime but tries to camouflage it as a normal and therefore necessary stage in the evolution of the species. At heart, modern society is fully aware of owing its origins and its civilized development to God but at the same time it knows that it has separated itself from God and it reaffirms its sacrilegious determination to remain separated from Him; it perseveres in its blasphemy. This goes by the name of secularization, dereligification. This is actually the desecration, in the fullest meaning of the word, of Christianity.

The parable tells us everything that happens afterward: dissipation of wealth in a spate of pleasure and lust, *"dissipavit substantium suam vivendo luxuriose."* That's the point we have reached now. A civilization that cuts itself off from God and holds Him off at arm's length can, for a time, create the illusion of abundance and facility, whereas it is really wasting, frittering away its strength, and the stench this produces evokes the end of the world — the end of one world, at least.

The next stage is an awful return to the truth of things: hunger and bondage, closely followed by beastliness. I'm not making this up; the Gospel tells us so. Famine having broken out in the land, the Prodigal Son fell into need and went to work for a master who sent him to look after the swine. So great was his hunger that he envied the husks fed to those filthy animals.

And then comes conversion. Even for our impious society, I think we can assume this will come to pass. *"In se antem reversus, dixit . . ."* Here is what I imagine to be the inner monologue of our Prodigal Son:

"OK! We've killed God. Now the stench of His body is filling the air. We've gone very far away, believing that our human portion of the inheritance made us inexhaustibly rich. We have tossed away by the fistful the treasures of the Christian civilization which our ancestors had patiently built up amid repentance of their sins and the hope of the Eternal Kingdom. We do not believe in sin any more, we have washed our hands of it once and for all. And as for the Kingdom of the future, we have lost our expectation, even our very dream of it. This world, this earth and this sky—that is what we want to possess, for our very own, right now. Let us eat and drink and fornicate, let's go strolling among the stars or in suburban gardens, and tomorrow we shall die:

"When the time has come to go and join the dead.

"I shall have lived without a care and died without a regret. Are we wrong to do so? Not only do the Nobel Prize winners tell us we are right, but some amusing little priests are also interpreting the Gospel to suit us, and they've just about convinced us that the way the Gospel has been read up until now has been one long misunderstanding.

"Yet we are still not satisfied. Even supposing we traveled to the farthest planets, what good would that do? Unless our universe is split open from the top, it will always be our prison, no matter whether its dimensions are expanded a thousand or even a billion times. When we were in the house of God, in His gardens, everything to us was hope, because everything was a promise to us of a world to come, of which this one is but a fleeting image as in a mirror.

The civilization which our ancestors had patiently raised up was merely an outgrowth of their search for the Kingdom of God. We who have abandoned that search and that lofty ambition once and for all have also lost the possibility of even that outgrowth; we give the computers orders for our own fate. We are down to envying the swine their unspeakable pleasures.

"We have taken rebellion to its ultimate phase, to the murder of the Father and the glory of the parricide. Is the world any more livable for all that? Pollution is everywhere, in souls and hearts, in the body and the mind, inside and outside of ourselves, in the very water, the air of the sky, the entire earth. Our unhappiness itself is dishonored, befouled. We are thrown back on ourselves, our sterility, our impurity. By seeking out the superfluous, we have come to lack the most essential. Keep quiet, you demagogues of theology, you who would like to make us forget our anxiety and strip it of meaning! Was God a liar? Or is it we who have not stopped lying? A decision will have to be made, but someone has definitely been lying. It stinks here. It stinks of rot and lies!

"How quickly time goes by ... When I left the old house under the trees, I still loved joy and ripe berries. The whole world was readying for the feast. Since then it has been covered over with cemeteries. Millions of men, women, and children have starved to death behind barbed wire. 'We don't get the connection,' people keep saying to me; 'after all, it's not because God is dead that half of mankind is starving and war has spread like an epidemic.' I also forced myself to believe this, because it's so much more convenient, so much easier to live if you refuse all responsibility for what goes on around you and just keep your own feet dry, like a beaver. Now I know that the convenient explanations are illusory. Ever since original sin, which was the first parricide, human brotherhood has been almost impossible. Our world has become the world of Cain—'I am not my brother's keeper.'

"Now I can see it all very clearly; ever since I left my father's house I have been all alone. I have even lost my taste for myself. I despise myself, and that's the truth. The very words that have to do with honor are no longer anything but an undecipherable vocabulary. There is nothing left to love, nothing left to understand. The sense of veneration has atrophied until it has become nothing more than a frail, peculiar vestige, like a lizard's tail.

"Here I am living with the swine and not eating my fill; and if I stay here much longer, I will die of it. After all, suicide is catching, just like flu, and you can't cure the suicide virus with vitamins. The truth is that man cannot live without some hope that is bigger than himself. And if I have no more hope left, it's because I have lost the taste for hope!"

How long does a period of parable last in history, real history? A hundred years? Four or five hundred years? Hurry, Lord, hurry, in this latter part of the twentieth century, hurry before it's too late, hurry lest you be outstripped by the end of the world! May your reign recur!

We find the time long, but even so, things happen fast. Not so long ago Neitzsche (who died the very year this century began) was crowing over the murder of God—and now, here we all are, forced into collective suicide. The world of Cain is dominated by the temptation of suicide. This may be just an isolated incident, but it is enlarged to planetary dimensions, covering all of mankind. Nothing is less chimerical than the possibility of such a collective suicide. The ingredients are all there, all ready: famine, biochemical warfare, galloping birth rate, thermonuclear energy, all waiting for the death ray. We can safely say that ever since our age proclaimed that God is dead, its imagination in matters of death has reached the point of genius. It is true that if a scientist were to unleash the catastrophe, the end of mankind would still be a case of murder. But if an end were put to mankind as the result of collective despair, then this would amount to a collective suicide. But neither is there anything less chimerical for mankind today than an overwhelming epidemic of despair. If in the process of killing God we had acquired a taste for death and nothingness, then we would dispose of more means than we could choose from for putting an end to existence. Unless . . .

What? You don't believe that mankind, brought up
on atheism, drunk on eroticism, greedy for money
and immediate pleasures, is still capable of feeling
remorse, not to mention repentance? Well, I prefer to
rely on the parable rather than on your brief experience as dulled and satiated men. One day, and that
day is coming sooner than you may think, men will
be hit full in the face by a gush of something as
caustic as sulphuric acid—remorse first of all, then
repentance. Then men will stand up straight, and
deep down inside they will know that they are still
made for hope. They will burn what they adored and
will demand the keys to the Kingdom of God. That is
the moment the Church must live for; it must hold
out until then, for it is to the Church that men will
turn and demand the keys, and woe! if the Church
has lost them in the meanwhile.

That is why we are resolutely, once and for all,
opposed to any short-term, short-sighted revolution.
We know that man's destiny is not imprisoned in
time. We await another revolution, when the hope of
that Kingdom will alight once more upon our earth
like a bird, and the earth will rock like the deck of a
storm-tossed ship, like the deck of Rimbaud's *bateau
ivre*. Our Prophet is not Marx, nor Hegel, nor Freud,
but Rimbaud.

What else does the Parable tell us? Let's have a look at the end of it. Abjectly crouching in the pigsty, the Prodigal Son remembers the house of his father. "How many hired servants of my father's are in that great house? They at least lack for nothing while I am dying here of humiliation and hunger. It's too much! I will arise, I will go to my Father and I will say to him, 'Father, I have sinned against heaven and before yourself and am no more worthy to be called your son. Make me as one of your hired servants.' "

That's what conversion is. It begins with a clear-eyed scrutiny of oneself, with a judgment of oneself in relation to one's origins ("My father!") and one's ultimate destiny or vocation ("against heaven and before yourself"). And then an acknowledgment of one's own weakness, one's own betrayal ("I have sinned")—I have betrayed hope, betrayed my vocation. Just to remind the opportunistic little priests and the demagogical bishops once more that God's reconciliation with this world is absolutely out of the question until this world has been converted, until there has been remorse and repentance.

Undoubtedly it was necessary that the Prodigal Son sink so low, to such misery, to the pigsty; otherwise no such reversal could have occurred or even have been conceivable. It was out of the question in the midst of feasting and reveling, during the period of dissoluteness. The dissolute man has forgotten his origin and his vocation and cares only for the immediate present. Our society is still very far from repenting; it has just reached the end of dissoluteness, just reached the precarious point of waking up with a hangover and feeling, deep down in its innermost being, the shooting pangs of anguish. Blessed be that anguish! It means that in the wan pre-dawn, we are beginning to feel a little bit lonely.

Meanwhile, what does the Father in the parable do? This is where God's "politics," if we can call it that, is different—totally different—and altogether above any human politics, just as heaven is above the earth.

What would an earthly father have done? Either he would have hardened his heart, cursed his son, forbidden him to darken his door ever again, made it impossible for him ever to come home; or else he would have gone soft, pitied himself, told himself that everything could still be worked out; and away he'd have gone looking for his son, hiring a private detective, seeking his son in gambling dens and places of debauchery, struggling with him perhaps to prevent him from getting into trouble. Human, all too human! God never prevents us from getting into the trouble we want more than anything else to get into. He waits until we've gotten drunk on it, and then sobered up.

The Father in the parable does not do anything — doesn't enlist anyone's aid, doesn't telephone right and left, doesn't speak ill of his son, doesn't speak good of him either — he doesn't speak of him at all, just stays home with his sorrow. But from time to time he looks far away to the last bend in the road by which his son went away and by which he will come back if ever he is to come back.

If modern man is far away from God, as far away as the Prodigal Son ever was, it is because "they" have made us a world without God, a world where there is no room for God, and because we make do with that world. It's no longer worth going to the trouble of doing what one scientist did, who was foolish as only a man of science can be: namely, forbidding God to enter our laboratories. God hasn't the slightest desire to come into our laboratories. He is not in our computers either, or in our statistics or our opinion surveys. In a universe where everything — from atoms to the milky way—is organized and explained by science and technology, it is absolutely impossible to encounter God. From there to concluding that God does not exist is just one short step.

In order to discover—I won't even say God, but the possibility of God—it is indispensable to leave what is measurable behind, for that is just the point: if God exists He is, first of all, beyond measure. God can only be metaphysical. No point in looking for him anywhere else; and once you have examined everything that is measurable, isn't it marvelous to find that God is not there and so to conclude, triumphantly, that God does not exist! As if there were not, could not be anything beyond what is measurable. Luckily, there remains that anguish . . .

No matter what its immediate legitimacy and its historical necessity may be, the scientific conquest of the universe is, none the less, a dissipation of the soul, shutting man into forgetfulness of his properly divine origin and destination. There are no more timely words in all the Gospel than these: "For what is a man profited, if he shall gain the whole world and lose his own soul?"

Before he can do so much as think of God again, man must break out of his prison, with self-examination and remorse battering down the door, elevating him to repentance. "I will arise, I will return to my Father and I will say to Him . . ."

Here comes the Prodigal Son, tattered and dusty from the long road, trudging along as the defeated do, dirty and unshaven like a hippie coming back from Katmandu—here he is within sight of the paternal abode. From far away his Father recognizes him; his heart leaps up; he rushes out to meet his son, who has knelt down in the road. The Father lifts him up, kisses him, interrupts his speech, so that the son never finishes the plea he had been rehearsing over and over again on the way: "My Father, I have sinned against heaven and in your sight, and am no more worthy to be called your son . . ." In the joy of being reunited, there is no room for hired servants.

What follows immediately? The feast, the fatted calf, the musicians, a good soothing bath, sumptuous robes. The place of the Prodigal Son had remained empty. The past is not only forgotten; it is forgiven. And then the rest of the parable. There is no loftier

hope for the modern world than to know that some-
where, a place is empty and Someone is waiting ...
It seems to me that this is something the Church
ought to repeat to the peoples of this earth instead of
trying to tag along behind ideologies that are ever so
profane, and anyhow, quite worn out by now.

I realize perfectly well what seems shocking about
this parable: it is the fact that the price of God's
forgiveness appears to be man's defeat. And man is
not prepared to admit that he has been defeated.
Hence the revolt of pride, which rejects the whole
story, from the paternal authority to the fatted calf.
Is this legitimate? Draped in his pride, modern man
triumphs morosely. And *is* this a triumph, to begin
with? Cutting oneself off deliberately from one's first
origin and one's ultimate finality — that is plain
stupid; and stupidity is certainly the defeat of defeats
for man.

But acknowledging one's own limits, acknowledging as well the obvious limitations of the created
world, acknowledging that one is, oneself, contingent,
and a sinner too — that cannot be a defeat; for such
acknowledgment is inconceivable except in relation
to an absolute transcendency, access to which alone
ennobles man, providing the consummation of his
dignity as a free and intelligent being. In other words,
such an acknowledgment is an escape in itself. Es-
caping upwards is always a victory, even if you do
skin yourself a little in the process. Prayer is mere
chitchat unless, through the ardent fire of love, it
becomes an escape.

On the other hand, denying the divine fatherhood

of all creation means shutting up man in a blind fate, relegating him forever to a prison of which Christ's resurrection had broken the bars. Besides, if God is the Father of His creature because He is His creature's origin, He is still more the Father of it because He is the destination and the supreme finality of that creature. It is when he returns, and only when he returns, that the Prodigal Son discovers just how very legitimate the paternal love is, when that love has been consumed in forgiveness.

Who knows? Maybe it is true that mankind will enjoy "tomorrows that sing."

Part 3

Petition,
Addressed to the
Bishops of France

Reverend Bishops,

I n you are invested the dignity and the fatherhood of the Apostles, who saw and touched the resurrected Christ. I am not forgetting that it is the placing of your hands on my head which links me directly to the apostolic witness, that is, to Jesus Himself who, after overcoming death, caused Himself to be seen and seen again, touched and touched again, put to the test in a hundred different ways by those who were to become His witnesses. It is their witness which you are transmitting in this world—and as for the rest, neither you nor I care two hoots about it!

First of all, Reverend Bishops, I would like to recall a few self-evident truths, the kind that are called home truths, that dazzle by their irrefutability. The tokens of honor and in fact the honor itself with which the Christian peoples surrounded their priests and bishops for so long did not by any means stop right there, with those individuals, but rather, through those ordained individuals, were addressed directly to Jesus Christ Himself, of whom bishops and priests are the representatives, or images.

I remember when I was a young Dominican, not yet thirty, and had just been ordained as a priest, I went to Austria to visit my father's grave. At that time, the Dominicans wore their white habit even in the street. When I had finished celebrating mass and came out of the little church in a suburb of Vienna — a red suburb, a socialist suburb, where the church was merely an abandoned factory shed — the women and children were waiting at the door to kiss my hands. I very clearly realized that those women and those children wished to express their gratitude to God by kissing those ordained — yes, those holy, venerable hands which had just distributed to them the body of Christ, that body which is salvation. There where the body is brought, there shall the eagles gather, and not only the eagles but the doves as well. My hands no longer belonged to me; they were playthings in the quivering center of those flocking birds, whose language I did not understand.

It would have been grotesque to think that it was I, I personally, who was the object of that tender veneration. The truth is that I was so stunned by the joyous twittering and all those kisses on my hands that my heart was pierced through as by a sword, by the trenchant feeling of my own nothingness and at the same time by a feeling of the eminent dignity and infinite power which my priesthood had conferred upon me. Now I ask you: where in all that is there room for pride or vanity? On the contrary, the unfathomable disproportion between what I am and what I represent was so flagrant on that occasion that even today, the mere remembrance of it brings me face to face with the heavy responsibilities entailed in my ordination — and also with my infidelities and my sins. I blush to think that I am truly at the center of what I represent.

So I am not altogether certain, Reverend Bishops, that a refusal of the honors and the traditional tokens of honor — that this refusal, I say, always springs from the virtue of modesty, or that it expresses genuine Christian humility. Either the honors bestowed on us are meant, through us, for Jesus Christ, whom we represent — in which case, they can never be tender or touching enough — or else they are meant for our poor selves, in which case they are entirely out of place, and the acceptance of even the tiniest portion of them, no matter how minute, is an intolerable act of pride.

The truth of the matter is that we are going through a virulent iconoclastic crisis. We are being urged, and you too are being pressured, to get rid of all images of what is holy, all tangible representations of what is divine. Which accounts for the expulsion of statues from our churches. But is it really only statues that are at stake? ... We are refusing ourselves as images of God-savior-of-the-world, as representing God, representing Jesus Christ, supreme and eternal Pontiff, his Gospel, his Passion and his Resurrection. In so doing, not only are we feigning to overlook the tradition of the Church but we are also overlooking

the people themselves and their true nature. The
people love images. They love to love and hate
through symbols.

My career in the Church began in 1925, at the
Grand Séminaire de Saint-Flour, whose Superior at
that time was Father Salièges. I wore a cassock, and
wore it everywhere, as was customary in those days.
At vacation time I went to stay with my mother in
Clermont-Ferrand. There was a good deal of working-
class anti-clericalism about then. Sometimes, as I
strolled through the outlying districts, youths my
own age "croaked" at me as I went by: cawing like a
crow had become, since the turn of the century, a
standard way or expressing dislike for a priest's black
cassock — which Maurice Barrès had drolly styled
"the uniform of lofty preoccupations." Such was the
spirit of the times.

I ran at my insulters, and that was enough; we
never came to blows. All was as it should be, it
seemed to me. I did indeed wear a uniform and I
accepted the historical and social liabilities that it
represented just as candidly as I accepted the honor.
For it was not I personally who was being insulted. If
I could accept the kisses on my hands in Austria, why
not accept the mocking crow calls — which pierced
me just as much.

Now, these are anecdotal trivia, you will say to me,
Reverend Bishops, and not worth dwelling on. We
belong to the same generation, and each one of you
could recall some minor incidents of the same sort.
But what I like is, precisely, to start with minor incidents and then expand the thought process and make

it open onto interrogations of a more serious nature.

To tell the truth, I am very much afraid that as far as our enormous task today — that of reconquering hearts, especially the hearts of the younger generation — is concerned, we have gone off on the wrong track completely. All younger generations have experienced soul-ache; it is the dignity of youth to call everything in doubt and be ill at ease. Today's youth is suffering, as anyone who has observed it from close up could tell you, from a metaphysical absence. What with masters like Hegel, Marx, Sartre, and Marcuse; what with the type of talk heard from modern scientists, whose intelligence, as everyone knows, very often flies at a low altitude since all it faces and supposedly overcomes is what is measurable, mathematical, what constitutes real or imaginary matter — which does not by any means inhibit them from holding forth peremptorily on things that are beyond them; what with all this, how do you expect modern youth not to feel sickened by the metaphysical void in which it is pent up? It's enough to make it vomit the contents of its soul as well as its belly—and that is what it tries its best to do, using drugs, eroticism, and disappointing trips into artificial paradises.

We alone would have been able, if not to fill up

that vacuum, at least to stock it with such a swarm of
questions, so intelligent, so mad and so common-
sensical at the same time, that the intelligence would
at least have remained upright and continued to seek
the light; and when the intelligence keeps on hoping
to understand, then the heart goes along too, and all
is saved. But we have repudiated the master of the art
of questioning, who was Thomas Aquinas. We
imagine we can reconquer the young by placing ourselves within their reach, by understanding them.
What does it matter whether we "understand" them?
It is our job to make them understand. Make them
understand what? Themselves, first of all; their destiny, their vocation, and also the world around them.
We cannot save them from themselves and the absurd
world in which they are plunged, but we do represent
Him in whom, alone, salvation is to be found.

By dint of de-mythifying, de-mystifying, de-
sacralizing, de-clergifying, trying to be like everyone
else, melting into the crowds, trying to be indistinguishable from the masses, by refusing to look at
problems from above and place them on the metaphysical level where they really arise, by examining
them only from underneath, from ground level, from
their Freudian or sociological or psychological slants,
we will leave unassuaged the anguish that we alone
could have soothed. We will be like the wicked father
in the Gospel who gave his famished child a stone
instead of bread and a serpent instead of fish.

For after all, when you come right down to it, Reverend Bishops, what we, in our iconoclasm, are in danger of throwing overboard is our chance of martyrdom. There is no martyrdom unless he who dies is killed out of hatred for the faith; in other words, he is killed not because of what he is but because of what he represents: God, revealed in Jesus Christ. What we represent in this world is exactly what we ought to live for and what we ought to be prepared to die for, if necessary. The indissoluble unity of our life and our death is forged by the cause we represent. In our case, it is no longer a cause but a Person, an adored, crucified, resurrected person, Jesus of Nazareth, born of the Virgin Mary, dead and buried in the time of Pontius Pilate.

We carry this burden — you, Reverend Bishops, far more than I do, and I have a share in it only because I have received it from you — of representing in the midst of the people Him for whom we live and for whom we would willingly sacrifice our lives. We can very well renounce the honors of this world, which would be meant only for our own persons, but we cannot—we have no right to, or else we would become the renegades of Our Lord Jesus Christ—renounce the honor which, through us, is due Him whom we represent. When such a burden falls on a man's shoulders, that man, whoever he may be, is doomed to that: to being the witness, the martyr if need be, of Him whom he represents, or else denying Him. There is no halfway point, no middle way, no neutral position.

There, Reverend Bishops!

Reverend Bishops, you are the shepherds guiding the flock. You are not the flock; you are the shepherds, the herdsmen, the pastors, not the sheep. I personally place myself in the category of the sheep-dogs — "Domini canes" — that round up the entire flock twenty times a day, sniffing and nipping at their heels, and must be ready to fight off wolves. For wolves there are and even, the Gospel tells us, mercenaries, which are no better. You are the shepherds. Your burden, your mission, your witness, your martyrdom if need be, is to be the images of the Supreme Shepherd, Jesus Christ, and the legitimate heirs of the first shepherds, the Apostles.

In that case, what are we to think of the tendency (I was about to say, the temptation) of such and such a bishop to characterize himself first of all — I heard this with my own ears on the radio — not as the representative of Jesus Christ and successor to the Apostles but as representative of the Christian community for which he is responsible? Only by distorting one's thought and one's language can one manage to believe and say that the shepherd represents the flock, at least within the framework of Catholic Christianity. Even when the bishops were elected by an assembly of the faithful, they were not consecrated, that is, made bishops, by that assembly. And because they are consecrated, it is not the faithful (the flock) whom they represent, but the eternal Shepherd, Jesus Christ. If by some mischance the bishops were to deny that they represented Him, it would be Jesus Christ Himself who would be deserting His flock. That is what the liturgy teaches us: *"Gregem tumm, Pastor aeterne, non deseras."*

The same applies to the Pope. At this time he is elected by the College of Cardinals. One may argue that he could be elected by a more extensive electoral college; this is secondary to the main purpose. His dignity as Pope is not to represent the electoral college from among which he was chosen but rather to be the Vicar of Christ, to administer the Person of Christ.

With all the respect which is due to you as successors to the Apostles, and because of that very respect, we give you a solemn warning, Reverend Bishops: what you have to say on behalf of the flock does not interest us in the least. If you speak on behalf of the flock, we are afraid we will hear only bleating. Now, we have known for a long time what bleating amounts to. It can't teach us anything, and still less guide us along the way to salvation. When Panurge's sheep rush into the sea, they bleat and bleat as loudly as they can.

In the Church, the good echo is the one that descends from above, not the one that rises from below. When you open your mouths, we expect to hear something other than bleating. We insist on hearing the echo of a Voice higher than yourselves, the voice of Him who said, "Whoever listens to you listens to me, whoever scorns you scorns me, whoever scorns me scorns Him who sent me."

This presupposes that you yourselves listen, above the bleating and trampling of the flock, to the Voice that comes from the Father through Jesus Christ.

"Whoever scorns you also scorns me"—that is meant for us, and we feel the responsibility it places upon us. But "whoever scorns me also scorns Him who sent me"—those words are meant for you too. If instead of passing on to us the voice of Jesus Christ and the voice of our Father, you merely echo the bleatings of this earth, you do not interest us any more at all and, what is more, you no longer have any right to insist on being listened to. We know the bleatings of the earth as well as you do, and even better; and we don't expect anything good from that quarter. We have read Rabelais.

We also read the Gospel. Even in the parable told by St. John, where the good Shepherd is tenderly attentive to his sheep ("I know my sheep, and my sheep know me"), we are always told that what constitutes the flock, what holds it together in its oneness, is not the bleating of that flock (flocks of sheep always bleat, even—especially—in the hands of mercenaries, even when attacked by wolves, even on the threshold of the slaughterhouse); no, what brings the flock together and makes it a peaceful one, is the voice of the Shepherd: "And they shall hear my voice, and there shall be one fold and one shepherd." That is the voice which you must pass on to us.

We can only beg you, Reverend Bishops, to read and reread this parable in the Book of John, and to weigh and meditate upon each word in it, to consider it as a whole and in detail. It is true that the Shepherd knows his sheep, each by name, the name in Paradise; It is true that at the sound of his voice, the flock leaves the fold to go into the pastures. But it is clearly said, not that the Shepherd accompanies the flock or goes along with it, but that he *goes before it: "ante eas vadit."* It is clearly stated that the ewes *follow* because they recognize his voice: *"et oves illum sequntur, quia sciunt vocem ejus."* All of that is very clear; shame on whoever tries to obscure its meaning, ever: it is up to the Shepherd to go before, to lead the flock; it is up to the flock to follow, and not just any old way, but by following his voice.

Reverend Bishops, we greatly fear to see this procedure carried through the other way around. Instead of the flock knowing and heeding the shepherd's voice, it is the shepherd who would listen to the voice of the flock and obey it; instead of the shepherd going before and his flock following behind, it is the flock that would drag the shepherd after it—or, in these familiar words, which have been at the origin of so many disasters: I *must* follow them! After all, I'm their leader!

Following the example set by the Master of us all, you should be prepared to give your life for the flock which is placed in your charge, but your duty is to know how to talk to it as an echo of another Voice far above yourselves, to walk ahead of the flock and not follow it or even go along with it, lost and indistinguishable in the mass. That is the truth about your vocation as bishops, your mission, your function, your usefulness in the Church. Such is the truth of the Gospel, where you are concerned; outside of that truth, you would be nothing and everything you could say to us would be wind.

Nor are you the spokesmen of a human community; you are like the Prophets; you should utter the words which God and Christ place in your mouth and on your lips. When you claim to be speaking on behalf of the human community, you the spokesmen of God, the effect on us is a strange one, as if a flock of ventriloquists was bleating through your mouths. It is insulting for us, humiliating for you, injurious for Our Lord Jesus Christ. One gets the impression that the Church has become a haunted house, filled with inexplicable noises and strange words. One does not feel nearly so much like listening to you as like reciting one's rosary and telephoning to whatever exorciser happens to be on duty at the time.

Get it clearly into your heads, Reverend Bishops, your heads and your hearts too, that your power and your prestige over us, that make us lend you a respectful and attentive ear, come from the fact that what we expect to hear from you is the word of Christ, and not the bleatings of the faithful. Even if you were elected by the community, your power would come only from your consecration and from delegation by Christ, through the Pope. You are not a branch of a democracy, not at all; you are a particularly important and honorable echelon in a hierarchy which descends from God to men.

When talking about the Church, I do not like the words monarchy and democracy, because those words have been devalued too much to designate so strong and precious a reality. I prefer to refer to Thomas Aquinas' commentary on the passage from Saint Paul: "You are fellow-citizens of the saints and of the household of God," and to consider the Church a clan whose Patriarch is God and whose Eldest Son is Jesus Christ. And the Pope is the Vicar of that Christ, and you are his lieutenants. That's where your legitimacy comes from. Outside of that line which descends to us, the flock, we do not even have the right to heed and obey you. In the name of what would we do so?

It is true that the Church is also, when looked at on a horizontal level, a City, the City of the saints, where the distribution of wealth is achieved, not by social justice, but by a generous exchange of acts of faith, hope, and charity, for in this City what belongs to one belongs to all, and all belong to God.

There has recently been a great deal of debate over the very topic of this book: God and politics, or to put it another way, Church and State. I have followed these debates closely and objectively, and I have found them disappointing, and not always very honest. After all, it would be only elementary honesty, when participating in such a debate, to quote from an apostolic text which is as appropriate, in this case, as it is famous. I mean Chapter XIII of Saint Paul's Epistle to the Romans. Whether one likes this text or not, one has to be familiar with it; it must be brought into the discussion, especially if the discussion is conducted publicly, in front of millions of television viewers or radio listeners who are interested in the subject but who have no special reason to know this particular text or realize what an exceptional amount of authority it carries in this context. For it is indeed an apostolic text, part of the Apostles' heritage, which was passed on to you.

That text is impressive. Here it is: "Let every soul be subject to the higher powers; for there is no power but of God and the powers that be are ordained by God. Therefore whoever resists that power resists the established order of God, and shall receive to himself damnation. For rulers are not to be feared when one does good works, but only when one does evil. Do you wish not to have to fear power? Then do good, and you shall be praised for it, *for the ruler is the minister of God to you for good.* But if you do evil, then be afraid, for he does not bear the sword in vain; he is the minister of God, a revenger to execute wrath upon whoever does evil. Wherefore you must needs be subject not only for wrath but also for conscience sake. Is it not for that reason that you pay tribute? For the rulers are God's ministers, attending continually to this very thing. Render to all their dues:

tribute to whom tribute is due, custom to whom custom, fear to whom fear, honor to whom honor."

There you have, very clearly put, the apostolic doctrine on the relationship of Christians to the State and politics. The context is very eloquent. The Emperors in the time of the Apostles were no paragons of virtue and liberalism; their names were Tiberius, Caligula, Claudius, and Nero. This makes Saint Paul's words all the more forceful, and it is better so. In the Apostle's opinion, the obedience due to the civilian authority does not strictly depend on the virtues of the person wielding that power but, rather, on the nature of that civilian authority, which is an instrument of God to lead the multitudes to a certain good.

At any rate, there can be no question, for us, and still less for you, Reverend Bishops, of rejecting or forgetting this important text. We must try to understand it but first of all we must accept it straight away, both the spirit and the letter of it; there can be no camouflaging it. At first glance, there would seem every justification for concluding that the Church is against any kind of challenge to authority, any kind of disobedience, and even more strongly against any upheaval—in short, that the Church, in its essence and by its foundation, is an institution with politically and socially conservative aims. But it is not as simple as that.

The task of the Church is, essentially, to bear witness in this world to what lies beyond this world. Its task is to open minds and hearts to eternity. Its supreme ultimate end is not of this world; it teaches all men that this world is only a passage, an intermediate state, a stage through which they absolutely must go in order to reach their genuine destination, in the hereafter. To men who, partly out of pride, tend to look upon themselves as mature, complete men, as adult beings, the Church teaches that with respect to their Creator and their final destiny, their autonomy is only an illusion, that their life at present is only an embryonic condition, that for the time being they are merely fetuses who are soon to see the light of day—but that light lies on the other side of the world. What would a fetus be if it did not aspire to be born? For a fetus there is no such thing as a third solution: either it moves towards its own birth and toward a light of day it does not yet know, where it will develop and finally, fully become itself; or else it is altogether satisfied to be a mere fetus, is perfectly comfortable that way, feels quite grown-up and wants to remain like that—and the end of it all is a miscarriage, flushed down the toilet.

True enough, the Church does, insofar as it is faithful to its supreme finality, abandon the management of the political affairs of this world once and for all, which does not mean that it has turned away from them entirely. In the earliest days of the Church, this position was legitimate and sincere—heroic, even, and altogether new. What was revolutionary at the time was the fact of splitting the conscience into two by solemnly affirming that man owed allegiance to two authorities, that each of these was autonomous in its own sphere and that the one was none the less subordinate to the other, since the temporal authority was to respect the indefeasible rights of the conscience and the one God. The Church was actually renewing the story of Antigone's heroic dilemma.

If there is but one God, creator of heaven and all the earth, and if all authority, including political power, flows from that God, then it is beautiful and imaginative, and also extremely courageous, to maintain on the one hand that the duty of adoration cannot be shared and is due only to the true God, to the exclusion of Caesar himself, and on the other hand to insist just as solemnly on the duty of obedience to Caesar, in the political sphere, even when one is persecuted by the very authority whose legitimacy one recognizes. At all events, this attitude was the opposite of opportunism, and in it is the source of that admirable ambiguity—the double allegiance—in the Christian conscience, which delivers us forever from the earthly dreams of the Old Testament.

What happened? In so fiercely monolithic and totalitarian a world as the Roman Empire, where everything—bodies and souls, earth and heaven—belonged to Caesar, the statements made in Genesis and the Gospel could not help but have even political consequences in the long run. But those consequences emerged very slowly, shaped by a long and natural process of gestation; and insofar as we do in fact remain faithful to the Christian teachings, in all their complexity and their transcendency, then we have not yet finished discovering new and even political consequences of that fertile, outstanding doctrine.

The pronouncement in Genesis, for instance, that God is the sole creator of heaven and earth could not fail to have far-reaching effects upon property rights, exercised as they were, within Roman society, in an unreserved and implacable manner. Property rights became relative, subordinate to the previously established and indefeasible right of God the Creator. Berdayev emphasizes the extent to which this conviction—that the earth belongs to all since it belongs to God in the first place—imprinted itself upon Russian Christianity and partially accounts for the success of land collectivization in Russia. There is a relativity of economic organization which is embodied in the Christian heritage. Unfortunately, there is nothing relative about today's Communism; it is an atheistic monism.

Similarly, the unimpeachable dignity of the laborer stems from the fact that all labor participates in the divine creation. God created men as creative beings, and God's creation is continued and expressed in the labor of men.

Or again, when one asserts that man, any man, is created in the image of, and resembles, God, one bases human dignity on that original and inalienable relationship and thereby brings an element of relativity into all social distinctions, by class, nation, age, or sex. The veritable basis of human dignity lies beyond all of those distinctions.

As for Jesus Christ himself, He violated all the

rules. He carried His heroic obedience to his Father and His love for mankind to the point of madness. As so many saints have demonstrated—a Joan of Arc, a Francis of Assisi, a Benoît Labre, for instance—the children of God enjoy a prodigious degree of freedom when they are totally devoted to imitating Jesus Christ.

Reverend Bishops, the task of the Church in this world is to produce saints. We do not ask anything else of it, but that much we are entitled to demand of it. Perhaps we still have too conventional an idea of saintliness. Let's say that we ask the Church to produce free men—men who are free in relationship to themselves, first of all. Although recommending commitment is meaningless, on the other hand a Christian is always bound to try to rise above the lusts of the flesh and to rank his duties in hierarchical order: "Service to God first!" said Joan of Arc, yet we know how far she carried her temporal commitment.

With that in mind, the permission which is given us to be a little bit socialist—a little bit, not too much—following upon the recommendations that we should be Christian-democrats, offers a hint as to the distinctions that will soon be made, to help our consciences rally to Communism or Maoism. . . . One can't help smiling at all that. Produce free men, and they in turn, where their temporal obligations are concerned, will manage very nicely without your permissions and recommendations and your distinctions. A marvelous saving of time and prestige for you, Reverend Bishops!

I have known some free men. Bernanos was a free
man, because he was Christian. He was extremely sub-
missive to the Catholic hierarchy when it taught him
the Gospel and dispensed the sacraments, but he did
not expect anything else of it. Reread *Grands
Cimetieres sous la Lune,* Reverend Bishops! De Gaulle
was a free man. As for President Kennedy, he had
become one. At the time of the Cuba crisis, he sought
the advice of a theologian in whom he had con-
fidence. He wanted to know whether he had the right
to run the risk of starting a universal conflagration.
The theologian drew up a long, detailed report which
raised more questions than it settled—and arrived two
weeks after the crisis had been resolved. The President of the United States had had only a few hours
in which to make his decision and in the end he had
to decide alone. But it was he, after all, who was
President, he who had the responsibility, and the
grace.

When I think about the relationship between the
Church and the State, or about the conduct of clergy-
men in politics, I am reminded of this maxim of
Pascal's: "Domination that overreaches its realm is
tyranny!" That is valid for both sides of the barricade—if barricade there be.

W hat we call "revolution"—that is, the effort to change life and upset society, in order to make them fit an ideal of freedom and brotherhood—could not have been born and developed outside a Christian climate. Within such a climate, revolution acquires an eschatological echo of repentance, atonement, and even conversion. Christianity planted within society a ferment of dissatisfaction and discord, in the etymological sense of *cor,* which means *coeur,* heart. Christianity rends and shatters the heart, which is torn between eternity and time, between loyalty to God and political loyalties. The Christian Apocalypse perpetually questions the validity of everything, endlessly challenging what is temporal in the name of imminent eternity. It is this climate of divided hearts that leads into a revolution when suddenly the validity of all society is questioned, not in the usual way—in the name of eternity —but instead, in the name of a utopia that has dressed up in the flashy finery of the absolute.

We can easily understand, Reverend Bishops, that having served the established authorities so often, you are now willing to look indulgently upon the revolutionaries' arguing and questioning. May we merely beg you to be careful not to be too hasty in separating the chaff from the grain, not to be in a rush to decree which is the grain and which is the chaff that should be burned, not to usurp ahead of time the function of rendering the Last Judgment which Christ set aside for Himself and which belongs to Him personally—in short, not to compromise the Gospel and your lofty functions in an argument which may not be on a purely spiritual level, which may in fact mask a lunge to grab power.

Are you sure that today's political disputes have not already contaminated the way the Gospel is preached? The Lord's Commandments and the seven deadly sins are talked about less and less. Theft is reproved only when it involves abuses of high finance and property—as if this particular sin were reserved to a single class of society. No one talks about envy any more, although it is such an ugly sin and causes so much harm. But people do get drunk on talk of social justice—forgetting that the foremost Christian virtue, after all, is still charity. Worst of all, no one nowadays ever talks about the outstanding position of dignity which the poor occupy in the Church; no one ever quotes those singular words spoken by our Lord on the day before His Passion: "For you have the poor with you always, but me you have not always!"

This passage is one that some people would like to erase from the Gospel. What is this nonsense about the outstanding dignity of the poor, when the aim of the revolution is to do away with poverty, not to honor it. The aim of the revolution is to redistribute worldly wealth, to see that everyone becomes rich, to keep the poor outside of the walls, like lepers in the old days, to wipe out poverty in the midst of the new City.

The odd thing about these words is that Jesus spoke them in order to settle a dispute that had arisen between Judas and Mary Magdalene. She had just poured over the Lord a perfume, or ointment, that

was worth a fabulous sum, in a gesture of pure prodigality and sumptuous tribute in the spirit of a funeral
celebration. "Outrageous waste!" grumbled Judas
("*Ut quid perditio haec?*"), when such a perfume
could have been sold for a very substantial price and
the money distributed among the poor. Today our
ears are filled to overflowing with examples of this
type of reasoning. Judas is a very modern character.

Jesus firmly reminds Judas and all whose mouths
are oozing with social justice that the first duty of
those who have understood who Jesus is to pay
tribute to His redeeming, sacrificial love. Besides, it's
true: any society will always have its poor people
(who are not always the people one thinks they are).
If you deprive these poor people of Jesus Christ and
the hope of eternal life, you make desperate people
out of them.

No, the poor are not always the people one thinks
they are. In 1945, when France was liberated, a confusion arose which proved immeasurably advan-
tageous to the Communist party, because the poor,
whom the Gospel speaks of, began to be identified
with the working class. Now, this is a monstrous and
abusive identification. I do not mean to say that the
workers are rich; but unfortunately, there are people
far poorer than the workers: elderly persons who are
neglected, abandoned children, people with tiny pen-
sions gobbled up by inflation, many lonely old men
and women, ill or crippled or retarded or isolated
people, prisoners, generally speaking, all who live
without hope or any means of expressing themselves,
who are not supported and aided by any social organ-

ization, any powerful association. These are the poor,
the really poor, and there may very well be middle-
class people among them. A man or a woman on the
verge of committing suicide is poor, no matter what
level of society he or she comes from.

But by dishonestly identifying the poor, in the
meaning of the Gospel, with the working class, it was
possible to go one step further, identifying the Beati-
tude of the poor with Marxist Messianism: "Blessed
are the poor, for theirs is the Kingdom of Heaven!"
Many young Christian simpletons dashed headlong
into the revolutionary "crusade." Franco's crusade
was a monstrous thing, and this new Marxist-Leninist
crusade is just as monstrous. The wolves are not the
same, but these Christians are running in just the
same way to go and join in the wolves' howling.

The mysterious, supernatural meaning of all the
Beatitudes must be safeguarded. The Beatitudes must
be kept open to all men of good will, all who are
truly abandoned and who cry, like Christ on the
cross, "Father, into Your hands I commend my
spirit." I do not place it in the hands of Marx or Mao
or Marcuse or any other pedagogue; only into Your
hands, Father, do I commend my spirit.

No one, Reverend Bishops, will reproach you
—quite the contrary—with feeling a special

tenderness or even an irresistible leaning for those whom society rejects, punishes, or neglects. But please do not choose your proteges: the most pitiable are those who should make you feel the greatest pity.

When we see one or another of you fall in with the line of action laid down by some union, we can't help wondering whether you have altogether lost your taste for consorting with the mighty. For in the last analysis, a labor union or party looks very much like the young Louis XIV, aspiring to attain his majority, become the State and be crowned King. It has its courtiers already. When Pope John XXIII went to celebrate Christmas mass in a grim Roman prison, that was not the act of a courtier.

If you remonstrate from time to time with the government, that is part of your role, and no one will criticize you for doing so. One short episcopal letter from Archbishop Saliège of Toulouse was enough to bring him glory. It was directed against the Germans and against a Préfet of the Vichy government. He was quite alone, Archbishop Saliège was, and so were the unhappy people he was defending. These people were the Jews, and the time was 1942. You remember, don't you, Reverend Bishops? Here is how his letter went:

"My very dear brothers, there is a set of Christian morals. There is a set of human morals that lays down duties and recognizes rights. Those duties and rights are based on the nature of man. They come from God. They can be violated. But it is not in the power of any mortal being to do away with them.

"That children, women, and men, fathers and

mothers should be treated like some lowly herd of animals; that members of the same family should be separated from one another and shipped off to some unknown destination—it was left for us, in our own day, to witness these sad sights.

"Why doesn't the right of sanctuary in our churches exist any more?

"Why have we been defeated?

"Lord, have mercy on us!

"Our Lady, pray for France!"

Here we have the tone of *Antigone!* Here we have the tone of a French archbishop speaking amidst the danger threatening his flock! I repeat that this letter was written in July 1942. If only Pope Pius XII, who knew as much as Salièges did, and even more, had spoken out in the same terms, what repercussions his attitude would have had. ... Luckily Salièges was there, through whose voice the Church of France and in fact the universal Church raised their own voices in protest. In times of great peril, all it takes is one bishop, just one, amidst the general silence, to make the executioners shrink back and restore hope to those who are miserable. Reverend Bishops, what a great responsibility you have! One bishop, just one, who knows what he's saying and says it well—what a resounding bell of alarm he rings, the world over!

That is just what Saint John Chrysostom says, in the homily we read in the Mass for the Doctors of the Church: "Look closely at what is said, 'You are the salt of the earth.' It is not of your own life only but of all the universe that you shall have to render account! It is not to two cities only, or to ten or twenty cities, or to a single nation, that I send you, as I sent the prophets, but to all the earth and all the sea as well, to all the known world, this world bowed down with crime!"

B ut things are always a little more—I won't say complicated but, complex than one suspects they are. It is true that, as a successor of the Apostles, a bishop has a universal vocation and a universal responsibility. But that universalist vocation could provide an alibi concerning nearer, more immediate responsibilities. To make my meaning clear, I will complete what Saint John Chrysostom says with the parable of the good Samaritan. Reverend Bishops, may I give you my interpretation of that parable?

A man was on his way down from Jersualem to Jericho. Attacked by highway robbers, he was wounded, robbed of his valuables, and left by the side of the road in a pool of his own blood. A priest goes by, turns away, and hastily continues on his way. Where was this priest going in such a hurry? To an anti-American, anti-war-in-Vietnam rally! In the same way, a Levite happens by and turns hastily away; he was going to a protest meeting against the Burgos trial of Basque nationalists, or the civil war in Pakistan, or the one in Biafra, or what have you. At all events, both the priest and the Levite had their hearts full and their minds taken up with things going on thousands of miles from the poor devil who was dying right there in front of their eyes. Isn't it marvelous that the call of those great—and distant—causes, that we can do nothing to change anyway, can make us feel justified in doing nothing for those who are within reach and whom we could and should help.

I am not saying that the problems of the underdeveloped countries are not our problems too. But I fear that the grand statements and manifestoes that are published on those subjects actually camouflage a great deal of hypocrisy. Addressing the Left-Bank intellectuals of Paris, Malraux noted, "If you take a stand against the dictatorship in Bolivia, what do you do? Leave for Bolivia? or head for the Café de Flore?" I cannot forget that there is one bishop in the Church who has taken an absorbing interest in the developing countries, namely, Cardinal Leger, Archbishop of Montreal. He was covered with honors and headed one of the wealthiest dioceses in the world. What did he do? He resigned from his post as Archbishop of Montreal and applied for a post, not even a ranking one, as a missionary in Africa. Reverend Bishops, let us salute this bishop's devotion to the developing countries. There's a serious man for you!

Let's go back to the parable. The good Samaritan comes along. In Christ's day, the Samaritans were a much-scorned people. They did not belong to any parish or diocese; they were the gypsies of the Kingdom of Heaven. Nothing good could be expected to come of them!

And yet it is the Samaritan who stops, bends down

over the poor man, bandages his wounds, lifts him up onto his horse, takes him to a hostelry, takes care of him, pays for him—saves his life! Perhaps this good Samaritan was rather stupid. He was not a doctor of theology or of canon law, or even of medicine. He had a heart that could be moved to pity. Yes, he certainly was pretty dumb. He didn't even ask the poor guy who'd been robbed what union he belonged to, or what political party; he didn't even question him about his social status or his race or his nationality. In short, this good Samaritan was definitely not in the historical swing of things. And yet it is his action, Reverend Bishops, that the Gospel recounts as an example to us. *"Medita hoc!"* as the incomparable Cardinal Cajétan used to say.

To come back to Cardinal Salièges: you will notice, Reverent Bishops, that he was playing the role of the good Samaritan to the hilt since the facts he was denouncing did not concern something that had happened thousands of miles away. Apparently any appeal to the universal conscience must be rooted very deeply and, just as with trees, the deeper its roots go, the better the chance that its branches will reach very far into the sky. See how Salièges rises up from his little corner of the Church to launch his appeal, all of a sudden, to the furthest reaches of the horizon:

"Within our diocese, in the deportation camps of Noé and Récébédou, scenes of terror have taken place. Jews are men, Jewesses are women. It is not right that anything should be done to them, done against these men and women, these fathers and mothers. They are part of the human species. They are our brothers just as so many others are. No Christian can forget this."

One would like to see this letter included in the anthologies studied in the schools.

And France, Reverend Bishops, what do you think of France?

How far away are the days—and yet they were only a quarter of a century ago—when Cardinal Saliège could conclude his admirable letter in these terms:

"Oh France, beloved mother country, France, who instills into the conscience of every child the tradition of respect for the human person, chivalrous, generous France, I am certain that you are not responsible for these horrors!" And the Archbishop of Toulouse concluded, addressing all his priests: "To be read next Sunday, without comment." One French Préfet forbade that the letter be read. But many French priests, in their pulpits, read it aloud anyhow!

Yes, those days are long since passed. It is no longer fashionable to love France and still less so to admit it and talk about it, the way Saliège talked about it. It's the opposite that is fashionable now. Little shavelings talk to us in peremptory tones about "irrelevant, anachronistic borders." We who are no longer quite so young—you yourselves, Reverend

Bishops, and I, your humble servant—we owe it to ourselves to be more prudent, especially in a country where everything, and also the opposite of everything, happens so fast.

Just remember! When we were little, it was within the Catholic Church that one was a patriot, "Catholics and Frenchmen always." It was the people on the other side who were, simultaneously, anti-Catholic and anti-French; it was they who defaced the monuments to Joan of Arc and flung the French flat onto the dungheap.

But then the wind shifted. The passions changed sides, as has so often happened in the history of our country. The political cards were reshuffled and dealt again. What had happened? Simply this: France had been overcome, pinned to the ground, stripped of everything, including honor, left alone and bloody and miserable, left to die by the side of the road, just like the man in the parable who was attacked by brigands on the road that goes down from Jerusalem to Jericho.

You remember that, Reverend Bishops! How many priests and how many Levites went by, oh so quickly, without stopping, drawn on by the seven stars of the only constellation that was still shining in our dark night—the insignia of Marshal Pétain. Alas, their glimmer was misleading . . .

Who, then, stopped to succor France, bandage its wounds, lift it up and set it on its feet, keep hope alive, bring the country back into the battle, guide it back onto the road of honor leading to victory? Oh, there were some Catholics who were also free men:

de Gaulle, first of all, in London, and in France itself
good fellows like Edmond Michelet, and here, there,
and everywhere that handful of Catholics who four
years earlier, had denounced General Franco's
crusade as an imposture. And in the hierarchy, who?
Cardinal Tisserant, prevented from leaving Rome; and
Salièges in Toulouse; and one or two others. That was
all. By far the majority of Church leaders and their
followers rushed headlong into the Pétainist idoltry.

The rank and file of the Resistance fighters came
from the opposite shore—from among those who for
twenty years had been glorying in their pacifism and
statelessness, those on whom one really had no right
to count at all, and also the communists, the an-
archists, the rabble. As always, it is among the rabble
that you will find the best Samaritans.

We have never reproached the Catholic hierarchy
with not having joined the Resistance. We have reproached it with having taken up with those who
were on the other side—and who, in turn, had taken
up with the enemies of our country. We have reproached it with not having left us free and in a position to do what our consciences ordered us to do.
Even if a priest, and especially a bishop, has personal
preferences, he must keep his priesthood freely accessible to any and all, even to the enemy. When I was in
prison I was in contact with German chaplains, who
did their duty as priests toward me. I always tried to
do my duty toward their men. The priesthood
transcends wars and social conflicts, transcends all
causes dividing man against man, and does not place
any restriction on the service it owes to all.

With all the respectful anxiety of which we are capable, we say to you, Reverend Bishops: be careful! We would be so sorry to see you take sides once again—and it would be the wrong side, of course. You know perfectly well that Salièges and Tisserant were isolated examples during the Occupation; the main flock of bishops was elsewhere, had practically accepted the obliteration and humiliation of France, and was loudly confessing France's sins. Today we beg of you, don't start placing the same bets on the same kind of lame, one-eyed horse all over again.

No matter how acute the crisis which is splintering family life these days may be, still you would not dare, Reverend Bishops, to speak out against that natural institution or bet on its disappearance. One's mother country is doubtless a more vulnerable reality than one's family, since it is the work of civilization rather than of nature, although history and geography have helped to shape it. The mother country corresponds nonetheless to a deeper-lying, more tenacious need than is generally believed. In time of danger, the necessity of the mother country stands out with an urgency which is sometimes terribly intense. Is it not precisely with respect to such a reality that the Church should exercise its tender vigilance, precisely to the extent to which that reality is

precious and useful to all and at the same time precarious and exposed?

As in the decades between the two world wars, we
are now witnessing a tremendous defamation campaign against our country, in fact against the entire
social order, against any and all political organization,
any and all definitions of the common good. Such a
defamation campaign is generally the prelude to abandonment and betrayal on a major scale. Reverend
Bishops, we beg you not to enter into such a dubious
battle, not to dissociate yourselves lightly from
France and from obedience to the law. If it were to
undergo some new trying experience, France might
very well pay you back in your own coin and throw
you out on the church steps.

Oh, of course it desn't really matter whether the
Archbishop of Paris turns out to watch the Bastille
Day parade. Personally, I would prefer that he didn't,
since in that way he would be refusing to give his
support to the traditional but ridiculous—or quite
outdated, at any rate—slogan of an alliance between
the sword and the holy-water sprinkler. But the
parade on the 14th of July is a little like the Tour de
France—only one spectacular aspect of France. That
is not what I am talking about.

There are infinitely more important questions than
that, and we would be greatly obliged to you for
giving us clear answers to them.

—In Chapter 13 of the Epistle to the Romans, do
the recommendations—no, more than that, the
orders—which Saint Paul gives the Christians, to the
effect that they must honor the civilian authorities

and magistrates and obey the laws with respect to all that relates to the common good, exclusive of any idolatry, of course, do those recommendations and orders remain valid for Christians today?

—Do the notions of mother country and the specific institutions which regulate the life of the French people as a community appear outdated to you? or do you find that they are still worth being defended and honored by the French people?

—No matter how indulgent you personally may feel toward any category of citizens whatsoever and even toward the lost sheep, such indulgence and solicitude being part of your pastoral duties, do you acknowledge that systematic subversion, subversion for subversion's sake, is condemnable and places a multitude of innocents, for whom you are responsible, in great danger?

—In short, are you prepared to assume your share of responsibility for the common political good of this country and this nation?

These are clear questions, and there is nothing offensive about them. But how depressing it is to hear all of these problems taken up, on the radio or on television, without these questions ever being clearly put—and of course without their ever receiving any clear reply.

France, Reverend Bishops! Age-old France! That should mean something to you! as if a slightly absent-minded woman were suddenly being reminded that she has a child . . . . For the holy Catholic Church, which you head and represent, was very instrumental in the coming into the world and the growth of this country, France. Formerly you were called "Defenders of the City"—*Defensores Civitatis* —Defenders of the Fatherland. A beautiful word, "Defenders." The liturgy applies it to the Holy Spirit. You were the holy spirit, the inspiration of this country, and also its advocates, the servants ministering to its distresses, its consolers, the auxiliaries of justice and even more, the bearers of mercy.

It is not, cannot, be up to us to malign the past. We could not speak ill of it without denying ourselves. In order, moreover, to understand it well, one must love it. You nourished, supported, comforted the country in its infancy, you guided its first steps . . . .

It was only normal, of course, that once France had grown to adulthood, it should shake off your protection. This was not achieved without quarrels, without insults hurled on both sides, but by now it has been done, it is all over. The season of resentment and sulking is over as well.

But when one has played the maternal role in the birth and growth of a nation which the Church has played in the birth and growth of France, it would be abnormal, not to say monstrous, if all that were to crumble into mutual indifference. That must not and will not happen. Such indifference would be mere frivolity, and even cruelty, for in a nation like France, frivolity almost inevitably engenders cruelty.

Surely, Reverend Bishops, you are familiar with the law of ageing as it applies to any human society or institution. One takes one's place in history through the services one renders. Then, imperceptibly, one moves into the next stage, when privileges reward services. The last stage is that of frivolity: "Après moi, le déluge!" Now obviously, I am talking about institutions and collective entities, within any of which a given individual may remain in the service-rendering stage, while another individual may telescope the several stages and, having run through the first one, may already have reached the stage of frivolity.

It is clear enough that for a period of, oh, say about ten centuries, the French Church rendered the greatest services to France, so great in fact that the formation and the very birth of that nation would have been inconceivable without that Church. Then came, for the French Church, the time of privileges, and they were on the same scale as the services rendered—that is, enormous. That period lasted for several centuries, with the services dwindling and the privileges growing bigger. Please God, may the time of frivolous conduct on our part toward France never come!

P lease God, may we all make a prodigious effort, such as is always possible in the context of the human adventure, to reverse the fateful current and avoid frivolity, so that the Church of France can discover, not new privileges but rather, a new occasion to serve. In order to do this, we will have to begin by trying to understand and unravel what seems at first so confused.

For instance, Reverend Bishops, we are happy to see you refuse all privileges awarded by the nation. Who would not applaud such an attitude, befitting the evangelical humility? I would make one reservation, however: as I have said before, we do not have the right to renounce the honor due to our vocation by abdicating temporal privileges. The peoples need to pay us such honors, for they are not intended for us but, through us, for our Lord Jesus, whom we represent. Our humility must not be demonstrated at the expense of what does not belong to us.

Similarly, what does the very idea of relinquishing all privileges mean? It can signify two things. Either the Church of France wishes to be only a servant at the disposition of one and all, at the disposition not only of individuals and families but also of that community called France. Or it can mean that the Church of France wishes to loosen its ties with everything, doesn't care one whit about France, chooses among the persons in whose service it wishes to be, pampering some, scorning others and sentencing them without trial, ultimately taking refuge in frivolity.

Reverend Bishops, it would be worthwhile to issue

a clear statement of your position on this matter. One cannot help but approve and honor a social family which refuses to accept any privileges awarded by the nation; but one could not help but despise and loathe a social entity which stood aloof from the destiny of all the others and pledged itself to frivolity. "Après moi, le déluge!' is no Christian maxim, any more than the words that Cain spoke, "Am I my brother's keeper?" France would not pardon its Church, and would have a right not to pardon it, for cutting itself off from the destiny of the nation as a whole: wasn't Vaticanism detested, in our country?

The people of France would find it equally un-palatable if the Church were to be sucked in by a wave of internationalism, in which individual countries would be drowned. The people of France could not bear to see its Church become a stateless Church.

H istorically, there are precedents enough to induce us to act prudently and only after careful thought. There would be nothing new about French bishops today becoming profoundly indif-ferent to France—to the most living, the youngest, the most paradoxical aspects of France. Aside from Tisserant and Salièges, and perhaps Théas, the bishops of France scowled at the Resistance movement. "We cannot recognize what does not exist," I was told by Cardinal Suhard's secretary.

During the French Revolution, almost all of the bishops of France stood by their social class and emigrated; which was lamentable. It was the infantry, as it were, the lowest ranks of the clergy which continued, but clandestinely, to serve the French people. It was those same humble priests who kept religious instruction alive, administered the sacraments, and resisted the masters of the day, the Constitution Civile du Clergé which jeopardized the independence of the French Church. And it was those same humble priests who filled the prisons and the horrible prison-ships and went to the scaffold.

When Joan of Arc was sent to help France, which was in a very bad way, the bishops in the occupied zone were collaborators, of course. It was one of those bishops who judged and sentenced her ("Bishop, I die because of you!"). But even the bishops in the free zone did not look favorably on her. The Archbishop of Reims, Regnault de Chartres, who was counselor to that ungrateful Dauphin whom Joan of Arc caused to be crowned, detested the Maid of Orleans. He betrayed her constantly, even on the very day following the Coronation. It was he who made Joan of Arc's attack upon Paris a failure, and for her that was the beginning of the end.

So there would be nothing new about the French bishops as a whole standing aloof from the fate, and even from the mystical destiny, of France. But neither would there be anything new about God judging the matter in a different light. After all,

France has survived every one of the abandonments and betrayals that fill its history. In its survival and in the integrity of its vocation and its genius, France owes a great deal to Joan of Arc and nothing at all to bishops Cauchon and Regnault de Chartres, who were its enemies. France owes more to its unsubmitting little priests who, along with their people, remained faithful to God and the Pope, during the Revolution, than it does to the bishops, almost all of whom emigrated. And as for the last war, the only bishop inside of France whose name will be forever glorious was Salièges.

It would seem that at the times when their country is facing its gravest crises, there is a permanent temptation for the French bishops, taken as a whole, to dissociate themselves from the destiny of France, to emigrate either inside or outside of the country and, like the priest and the Levite in the parable, to turn their backs and continue on their way without stopping to help France when it most badly needs help.

Everyone acknowledges that we are going through a grave crisis right now, a crisis which affects both persons and institutions, in short, the crisis of a civilization. It is possible that France, thoroughly upset by this crisis, may be threatened by something more than abandonment. Just as the Archbishop Regnault de Chartres detested Joan of Arc and did everything he could to make her fail, so in the attitude of part of the young French clergy today, one feels scorn and relentless hatred toward the country as mother country. To their minds, "mother country" is an outmoded category. What makes them so sure of it?

Alas, ever since the Pope's infallibility was challenged, everyone has been eagerly affirming his own infallibility, producing a regular downpour of individual and anarchic infallibilities, no less peremptory for all that.

Reverend Bishops, I am afraid that France is being abandoned—the concrete France which is there, which exists, with its qualities and its defects, with, too, its astounding genius for renewing civilization, as proven so many times in the past, the France which is still useful and motherly—I am afraid, I say, that we are abandoning it in favor of a check that will bounce; for the modern revolutionary utopia requires one first of all to abandon and smash what exists, in exchange for a vague promise that is likely to prove deceiving.

We are likely to abandon more than France, perhaps: the Catholic Church's place in the sun. But, you will say, who is talking about a place in the sun? We would make do very nicely with a place in the shade. After all, didn't the original Church live for a long time in the catacombs? and yet it was the Church, the living Church, the pure and holy Church, the Church of the poor, the one to which we aspire.

Of course I am moved by such language. How many times, in my dreams, have I been carried back to those days, which we are idealizing perhaps, when the mere act of professing one's faith in the Gospel immediately involved an enormous risk, a matter of life or death, of martyrdom. What greater glory than to shed one's blood for Jesus Christ? Yet such an ambition can go unaccompanied by pride. It is not likely to concern itself much with the weak, as they would risk the worst sort of abjurations.

I f you will allow me, Reverend Bishops, I would like to insert at this point a short interlude on Georges Bernanos—who, during his lifetime, was scarcely in your good graces. What a pity you didn't pay more attention to him while there was still time. But after all that is the fate of all prophets: while alive, they are not heeded; they are not understood until after what was to happen has happened; and the only way they are loved is dead. When you know what Bernanos' posthumous friends are like today, you cannot help thinking how lucky those post-humous friends are that he is indeed dead.

In *Maurras et son temps,* Henri Massis quotes a letter from the young Bernanos; dated 1926, it is an admirable letter, and its prophetic lesson is still top-ical. "My friend," it reads, "a new modernist invasion is beginning, and you are seeing the harbingers of it. A hundred years of concessions and ambiguity have allowed anarchy to make deep inroads upon the clergy. The cause of order can no longer count on very many of those devalued, limited souls. I think our children will see the bulk of the Church's troops on the side of the forces of death!" Massis concludes, after this quotation, that late in the day, Bernanos betrayed his youthful convictions and went over to those whom he had scorned the most. Bernanos' writings, which "they" are obliged to make available to us (but in what tiny quantities), are enough in themselves to disprove what Massis says. Whatever my testimony is worth, I say that right to the end, Bernanos remained admirably true to himself, to his childhood and his youth, and that even just a few weeks before he died, he could once again have written and signed the same letter—the same, word for word—as he wrote to Massis in 1926.

But though Massis was wrong, his mistake was excusable. Many others have been wrong too, in all sincerity. During a television interview, the journalist who was questioning me asked—and he was merely repeating what many people believe—how it was that Bernanos, who had begun with rightist and royalist inclinations, had ended up as a Christian progressive. This badly distorted image that people have of Bernanos has been troubling me greatly since he died nearly a quarter century ago. I have given it considerable thought, and I gave the interviewer the fruit of my meditations.

Bernanos died without leaving a will. Through the chance circumstances of his death, his literary estate was seized upon by people whose position was very different from his own, but he did not know this. I do not want to go into detail on a topic which still upsets me terribly after such a long time. Suffice it to say that all who are familiar with the movement of ideas in France over the past fifty years were astounded to see the same man, Albert Béguin, gather up, in the space of a few months, such contradictory literary estates as those of Bernanos, Mounier, and Teilhard de Chardin. It was not possible to do this without betraying one or another of them.

For instance, I know very well that despite his liking for Mounier personally—for Bernanos was a kind and sensitive man—not once from the time he returned to France after the war until his death did Bernanos agree, though he was asked again and again, to publish even a single line in *Esprit* (the review which Mounier had founded), so that he would not compromise himself or lead his readers' souls astray. But it was in *Esprit* that immediately following his death, and for many many years, unpublished texts by Bernanos appeared. Of course this was partly for the sake of money, for Bernanos sells well; but also, and especially, there was a deliberate wish to pass off Bernanos for what he was not, to use him as a flag to obtain clearance for goods the mere odor of which sickened him. The same mishap would have befallen Jacques Maritain had he died before having time to write *Le Paysan de la Garonne*. To what use would *he* have been put? God, who protects his work, did not allow that to happen.

But Bernanos' work is even more clearcut. Whoever studies the things he wrote toward the end of his life, which are scattered here and there, will see just how true to himself Bernanos remained throughout, and how unfair to him it was to make him keep a certain type of company. This passage, concerning *Esprit*, as a matter of fact, was published on May 29, 1946:

"I am saying this because I believe it my duty to

say it, even at the risk of offending my dear Mounier, unpaid ringmaster of those horrid little performing dunces who refuse the world into which they were born but are not capable on their own of wanting another, since Marxism wants it for them, in their place, and not even in their name. They proudly turn their backs on the past; they flee the past but also the present; they flee from themselves. With eyes closed, they leap into an experiment with communism, the way a desperate man leaps out the window."

To close this digression—although it is not taking me away from my subject, as you must agree, Reverend Bishops—I will quote Bernanos once more, a text dating from October 2, 1946, and once again about *Esprit:* "What your horrid little performing dunces want—who are tormented by the itch-mite of Marxist dialogue and, in between pirouettes, take turns scratching each other backstage—what they want from the Church is exactly what the doctors and the scribes dared to demand of Christ. After all, the Jews too were waiting for an 'efficient' Messiah, and all they saw was a poor man . . . a poor weak man who wasn't even capable of carrying his cross all by himself, amidst the jeers of the crowd. The Church does not disconcert us any the less, I agree, but has God ever wanted it to attract us? There is a scandal of the Church, but does God want to put an end to that scandal? or will He merely, until the end, give every man of good will what he needs to get around it?

"You find that the Church's visage today repels more than it attracts—but what if the reason it repels is precisely that we are turning away from it, that we do not dare look it in the face, that our faith and our love are no longer reflected in it? The masses are straying away from the Church; I can see that. But does the Church need the masses? or do the masses need the Church?

"Idiots! You have allowed a civilization to form which is the enemy of man, and you are counting on the Son of Man to help you carry that experiment through all the way. While you had already forgotten about original sin, look how it has revealed itself to you through the atomic bomb . . . . Fools that you are! You wanted an efficient world, and now you've got it. Die happy! . . . And now there you all are standing around the Church, as the Jews stood below Christ on the cross: 'Come on, if you're God, prove it. Save yourself! Save us!' But the Church will not deign to answer your taunts any more than Christ answered the thief who was crucified with Him."

Following the rule that says you must always re-assert a principle just as you are in the process of violating it, Albert Béguin wrote that Bernanos did not belong to anyone. Right! And definitely not to those who took possession of him.

In closing this digression on Bernanos, I might add that the answer I gave for that television interview, as to the way in which Bernanos' work was exploited after his death by his posthumous friends, was cut out of the interview before it was shown to the public. By whom? At whose request? I never knew and doubtless never shall.

E very time I think of Bernanos, of that great soul, I am carried away. I was just now thinking · of Bernanos, sitting in the little parlour of the convent of Saint-Maximin, his two canes leaning within reach against the wall, and talking and talking about the Church and France that his heart was so full of, talking in that deep echoing voice that is betrayed so cruelly by the recordings we have of it. Léon Daudet called Bernanos, *"tuba mirum spargens sonum."* That great voice was in fact announcing the end of the world, in any case the end of one particular world.

So, Bernanos was talking: "You'll see, you'll see, in the end they will let everything go—everything, I'm telling you, and for nothing, without gaining anything in exchange. They'll open their hands and everything will escape from them, forever . . . ." He was talking about the French clergy, Reverend Bishops.

Somebody said . . . My God!, it was I who said, "After all, perhaps we do not have any other choice than that between a Church of the Pharisees and a Church of the Catacombs . . ." Bernanos' eyes flashed lightning and it struck me. The words died on my lips. I knew I was in for it, the thunder was going to rumble a shattering *"Tu quoque, filii"* right at me. And it did!

"Ah," he said, "you too! You are just like the others—ready to betray, ready to drop everything, and all for nothing, of course. Disgraceful! How dare you utter such a piece of foolishness! Slandering sacristy gossip! Half-cracked Christian-Democrat drivel! No! Do you hear me? No, there is not just a

Church of the Pharisees or a Church of the Catacombs! There was another Church and there still is—
our mother, who bore us in her womb and whom we
still have a right to and won't let anyone take away
from us, and that is the Church of the Crusading
Knights, 'without fear and without reproach,' that
won its place in the sun. In the sun, I say! And anyhow, why should the Church—our Church—hide?
First of all, the Church is the light of the world, and
the Gospel tells us it must be raised up very high so as
to light the whole universe, so that the humble can
see it from afar and arise and begin to march toward
that light. For that matter, the sun itself *is* the
Church! Never never never can it stand in shadow!
The next time you feel like saying something stupid,
my friend Bruck, just remember what I'm telling you
now!"

Oh, I remember all right! And how lucky I was to
have been bawled out like that. As a matter of fact,
no one who was not bawled out by Bernanos ten or
even a hundred times can claim to have been his
friend or been loved by him. Nor was that harangue
directed only at me. Reverend Bishops, let me hum-
bly hand it on to you. Accept it in the same spirit of
humility.

After all, why should the Church go into hiding? Why should it go down into the Catacombs and take refuge among the tombs, if it is not forced to do so?

We always tend to think that the times we live in are hard, that our problems are altogether new and the solutions to them must be new as well. But when we try to get to the bottom of things and judge the essentials, we find that in other times and other places the same situations have arisen, and there have been only two solutions, which history has since made very clear: either holding on tight, or letting go. One singular aspect, also to be noted, is that in certain eras of decadence, the intellectual class as a whole is tempted to let go, and communicates that temptation to those around it.

In the final decades of the Byzantine Empire, the intellectual class was made up of monks, priests and bishops, for the most part. The extent to which they were responsible for the ruin of the Empire was immense, probably decisive, for Byzantium no longer believed in itself, and it was they who had undermined that faith. But they were opposed, very fiercely opposed to anything that might have saved Byzantium: they were against the Roman pope, against the Latins (and not without good reason, alas!), and they very noisily challenged the authority of the Basileus, that courageous Emperor who waged battle on the ramparts.

Meanwhile, they decided it was pointless to defend the ramparts; they favored non-violence; they stressed the spirit of tolerance expressed in the Koran. For them, any way you looked at it, the Turkish turban was better than the Latin miter. At heart, deep down inside themselves, they were like some of us—they felt overburdened by the responsibilities of the double allegiance—allegiance to one's country, compatible with one's allegiance to God. They didn't think there was any harm in letting go, and giving back the keys to the city.

So, the keys to the city were given back. Islam won the day and imperilled the whole Christian, western world, squeezing it between Spain and the center of Europe itself. It's all very well to sneer at Charles Martel wielding his sword at the battle of Poitiers, or Don John of Austria at Lepanto; but it is thanks to those soldiers that we are still Christians, that you, Reverend Bishops, *are* bishops, that Notre Dame in Paris and the Cathedral in Reims are not mosques.

Just as they used to vaunt the Koran, so today's Christian pedants ardently brandish the works of Marx and Lenin, the little red book of Mao Tse Tung —simplicity itself—and the books of Marcuse, that ill-at-ease philosopher. They rave about them and say, Why not give it a try? By upsetting society, the Revolution would be giving the Church another chance, second wind, new structures. They're all ready to give back the keys of the city. Imposters! They take their hands off the controls and call that adventure! The trouble is, the responsibilities involved in the pledge of Christian faith, concerning the city and within the city, are too heavy for them. So they back down, camouflaging their maneuver with revolutionary boasting. They would rather hand themselves over, body and soul, to the Minotaur of the future, the totalitarian stateless State that will tell them everything: what they are and what they must do!

B efore I end this book, Reverend Bishops, there is one question I would like to ask you. It is one I often ask myself. Are we so very very certain that our period in history and our changing society are turning their backs on religion, that at the end of the road to which they are committing themselves there will be no more mysteries, no more sacraments, no more rites, no more hierarchy, no more revelations, no more of those ultimate outcomes that the old (I was going to say, the true) catechism, the catechism of our childhood, stressed so much: Death, Judgment, Paradise, Hell?

The more I observe our point in time, the more I become convinced of the opposite. People need—youth, especially, needs—the sacred element, and they are going to need it more and more. The young, therefore, unfamiliar with the sacred element that we already have, since we are more and more hesitant to talk to them about it, will create—are in fact already creating—a religion any way they can, by chance or mischance. Their religion is artificial; it is improvised and clandestine. It grows wild.

Without getting into genuinely great art—be it poetry, painting, dance, sculpture, or music—whose adepts use the language of religious devotion in speaking about it, whose masterpieces radiate throughout the world in monstrances of perennial beauty, we can note that erotic dances recreate a feast-day ceremonial, that choreographers label their productions "masses," that the sacraments of drug-taking paint a backdrop of artificial ultimate outcomes, where paradise blends with hell; that politics dreams up revolutionary tribunals that hand down last judgments; that violence and murder fill the screen, where death flows like water; that the "hippies" found Carthusian or Carmelite communities, far from our cities, where they wear crowns of flowers and sing to the strumming of guitars, and sometimes seek to purify themselves in the blood of human scarifices, groping for the path to ecstasy and raising on high their limbs that bear the terrible stigmata of dope-needle marks. Do you really find, Reverend Bishops, that people today are moving away from religion?

Quite the contrary. People are getting religion again, and getting it just as hard as they can. Only, we are not involved in this; it's happening independently of ourselves, and tomorrow it will be happening against us. The lawless young, ever more brutal, ever more eager for the unknown, given over to secret and terrible rites, will hunt us, pursue us, spit in our faces, humiliate us, brand our hands with red-hot irons, because we will have abandoned the truth of the sacred element that we still possess—our sacraments and ded-

ications and exorcisms and processions, the humble
and mysterious display of our Eucharist.

Yes, if we want to respond to the ambition of
youth, ambition as greedy as famine, if we want to
capture its enthusiasm, mobilize its fervor, then far
from removing the sacred element from the true religion, our task must be to affirm at all times its
sacred character, its sacred expression, and to do so in
the most pointed, the most trenchant, the most spectacular ways we can find. We shall probably have to
devise new rites, create a ritual which will appeal
more strongly to the modern sensitivity. Even so, let
us beware of silly, improvised, over-hasty innova-
tions. A liturgy that goes back to time immemorial
retains a magical prestige.

Yes, I said "magical," but don't throw your arms
up in the air for that. There is such a thing as a
"ceremonial magic," and Professor Lalande, author of
a famous dictionary of philosophy, wrote of it that it
"acts upon the mind by means of a ritual." There is a
very suitable definition of our ancient liturgy.

At bottom, Reverend Bishops, there are not a
dozen different ways to deal with the anguish
of the times. We are driven to become and to produce
saints. Already, a very long time ago, Maurice Barrès
had written: "The Church of France needs saints!"

That need has grown bigger and clearer. Believe me, Reverend Bishops, I am deeply aware of the humiliation of having to pronounce the word, saintliness. Of course, I personally do not have any right to give lessons. But whoever I may be in the sight of God, the mind must remain clear, it must place up high what ought to be up high and down low what ought to be down low, and the hand must write what the mind knows to be the truth. To become and to produce saints—that is the reason we were ordained. Anything else we undertake is merely a hoax.

Reverend Bishops, let's stop being smart-alecks. We'll never be smart enough to overcome the problems of the day. Besides, it is the peculiarity of our day to be stuck in a blind alley. The problems are so intertwined that there seems to be no way to untie the knot. Who, after all, can offer a solution to the population explosion, the under-development of the third world, the arms race, the encroaching pollution of nature? In the last analysis, whatever is said on this subject, here, there and everywhere, is simply so much blah-blah-blah. And anyhow it's none of our business; we're not made for that. We have to make a breakthrough, produce men who are burning with love. Yes, the fiery furnace of charity—there is our deliverance. And when the three children were thrown into the furnace, they began to sing.

"Look first for the Kingdom of Heaven . . . ." We have to go further than that. Our duty is not to look for that Kingdom first, but to look for that Kingdom only, exclusive of any other Kingdom. And if we really look only for this Kingdom, of which Jesus

spoke, its transcendance, its sacred character, unfore-
seeable, a Gift freely given and without repentance,
then the promise given will be kept, and all the rest
will be granted us in addition.

Imagination first of all, an imagination of the heart
on a scale with the misfortune of man and the sub-
lime human adventure. We shall speak words that will
touch hearts. We shall invent enchanted liturgies, to
the glory of the Word incarnate and the priceless
Body of Christ. The Church will cause unknown
dawns to illumine the world. The cross of Jesus will
radiate love. The saint we need the most is Francis of
Assisi, a madman, mad with love, a poet, with the
stigmata of the holy Passion on his hands and feet
and in place of the heart.

Then perhaps, and without having attempted to do
so, we will still captivate the people, as our Master
did, whose enemies call him the "Seducer"—
"*seductor ille.*" "Look," they said, "just look: what
have we gained? The whole world has gone away following him!"—"*Ecce mundus totus post eum abiit.*"

H ow that power to captivate must have
struck the first Christians, for they readily
depicted the Christ, our Savior, with the features of
Orpheus. Orpheus? Do you remember the myth,
Reverend Bishops? Orpheus, minstrel of Hades,

troubadour of the afterlife, musician of love, whose song ravished souls from the depths, whose enchanted flute charmed lions and serpents, gazelles and birds. The legend has it that even the trees uprooted themselves from the earth and the rivers left their beds and changed their courses in order to follow him. Such is the power of the cantors of the holy, to spellbind. Reverend Bishops, what are we to think of this power over the heart of men, who, Shakespeare said, are of the stuff that dreams are made of?

Reverend Bishops, what you have to say, and the fact that you know the way by which to enter eternal life, the power you hold to relieve this poor world of its burden of sins, the keys of the Kingdom that you hold—all of these holy realities for which you are responsible make you the possessors of a sacred charm, on which the whole of mankind may ask you to render an account, for it is for the sake of all mankind that you possess it, and if you do not exercise that charm, no one can do it for you. As for Jesus Christ, his parable of the talents warns us of what awaits us, when we come to appear before him.

Here I am at the end of this book. As there is every time, there is now the bitterness of the backward look: have I said everything I had to say, everything that men of good will were entitled to expect of me? Have I said it well? I have doubtless said some stupid things. Will my book do more good than harm? Have I not been too insolent? Or have I, on the contrary, blunted some sharp-edged truths? I have certainly not aimed to offend anyone. But the truths that need saying are like the battering-rams used in siege warfare: they are made to break down the fortress gates, crash!, while the tocsin booms.

It remains for me now, Reverend Bishops, to ask you for your benediction.

Les Calycanthes
1968-71